Memoir of
Pierre Toussaint,
Born a Slave in St. Domingo

MEMOIR OF
PIERRE TOUSSAINT,
BORN A SLAVE IN ST. DOMINGO

by

Hannah Sawyer Lee

Foreword by

Plinio Corrêa de Oliveira

SECOND REVISED EDITION

WESTERN HEMISPHERE CULTURAL SOCIETY

Front Cover: Photograph of Pierre Toussaint taken shortly before his death at age 87; Courtesy of Columbia University Columbiana Collection.

The Letters are from the archives of the New York Public Library. All are translated from the French, except the letters by Euphemie Toussaint and L. F. Binsse, which were written in English.

Western Hemisphere Cultural Society
P.O. Box 417, Sunbury, Penn. 17801

Second Revised Edition 1992
Printed in the United States of America

ISBN 1-8810-0802-9

Library of Congress Catalog Card Number: 91-68114

CONTENTS

PUBLISHER'S PREFACE

IN December of 1989, John Cardinal O'Connor began the canonization process for an early New Yorker named Pierre Toussaint. In August 1990 the remains of Pierre Toussaint were exhumed for verification and subsequently removed to Saint Patrick's Cathedral in the heart of Manhattan where they now rest. The *New York Times* reported on that occasion that the Church was already investigating several reported miracles by Toussaint. At that time, the publishers of this book knew nothing of this man, but this introduction occasioned great interest and a desire to know more.

During our quest to learn more about this man, we came across Hannah Sawyer Lee's *Memoir of Pierre Toussaint, Born a Slave in St. Domingo,* a book published just a year after his death by one who, having known him and having been moved by his virtuous and enchanting life, desired to make his life more widely known. But that was almost 140 years ago, and Pierre Toussaint is surely unknown to most Americans today.

Western Hemisphere Cultural Society, Inc.—a cultural and educational foundation deeply interested in researching and furthering the values our history has bequeathed to Christian civilization—takes pride in being able to bring the extraordinary and fascinating life of Pierre Toussaint to wider public attention.

The work presented here is essentially a revised second edition of Hannah Sawyer Lee's book, to which we have added a few samples of letters drawn from Toussaint's voluminous correspondence. We are fortunate also in having a foreword for the work from Plinio Corrêa de Oliveira,* the outstanding Brazilian Catholic leader who is justly world-renowned as a writer, polemicist, and untiring champion of Christendom.

In publishing this work, we hope to contribute toward Pierre Toussaint's canonization—while readily admitting that judgment of his sanctity is reserved to the Holy See—by sharing in the efforts to make his virtues known, for we believe he practiced these virtues with heroism as he faced the vicissitudes of this life doing good to others, ever a model of conformity to Divine Providence with his gaze firmly set on heaven.

While extolling Toussaint's virtues of patience, compassion for the sufferings of others, and the like, we certainly do not thereby praise slavery. The publishers, being Roman Catholics, look back with profound satisfaction at the historical record of the Church's efforts to mitigate the sufferings of slaves and eventually to eliminate slavery. In this vein, we cannot resist quoting from one of the last official documents of the Church in her battle against slavery and its evils:

"It is, however, chiefly to be wished that this may be prosperously accomplished, which all desire, that slavery may be banished and blotted out without any injury to divine or human rights, with no political agitation, and so with the solid benefit of the slaves themselves, for whose sake it is undertaken."

Thus spoke Pope Leo XIII to the bishops of Brazil in 1888.

This being said, we conclude here by affirming how profoundly attracted we are to the life of Toussaint at seeing how he accepted the cross of this harsh yoke with nobility of soul, with revolt against neither God nor men, but, quite to the contrary, making use of this undesirable condition to ennoble both himself and the society in which he lived and worked.

---

* Plinio Corrêa de Oliveira is a great nephew of Counselor João Alfredo Corrêa de Oliveira (1835-1919), who promoted the abolition of slavery in Brazil.

FOREWORD

T HE present biography of Pierre Toussaint appears at a good time in the United States.

His person, which in times past enjoyed deserving distinction in New York City, where he exercised the profession of hairdresser for ladies, has vanished from the memory of New Yorkers with the passing of generations, due to the dizzying pace of activities in that immense American city. But the examples he left during his life deserve to be remembered, for they bring about profound moral and social reflections for all times. These are highly opportune for our days.

The time in which Toussaint lived (1766-1853) was shaken, precisely like our own, by violent international events. The fundamentally atheistic French Revolution, which erupted in France in 1789 during the reign of the apathetic and indolent Louis XVI, has been deservingly qualified as the precursor of communism. This Revolution spread throughout France in a violent way and then spread to several European countries.

In 1794, when the appalling phase of the Terror came to an end, many hoped that the Old Continent would return to its former tranquility. Such did not happen. The Revolution, ceasing to be directly destructive on the material plane of facts, did not thereby cease to exist and spread itself more and more throughout Europe and elsewhere in the ideological field. In fact, the successive regimes of the Directory (1795), the Consulate (1799), and the Empire (1804-1815) were nothing but metamorphosed forms of the French Revolution. They were inspired by the same erroneous principles and consumed by the same desire to preach these errors to the whole world. Even when Napoleon, proclaiming himself emperor of the French, crowned himself in the church of Notre Dame in Paris (1804), his counterfeit monarchical regime was nothing but another metamorphosis of the French Revolution.

In fact, the order of things he imposed in France, peaceful in appearance, was nothing but the consolidation of the subversive modifications that the revolutionaries of 1789 had introduced into that country. On the other hand, wars of conquest waged throughout all of Europe, extending from Lisbon to Moscow and producing disturbances from Stockholm to Naples, enabled the emperor to impose revolutionary laws wherever he went, thus subverting the old order in the name of the principles of liberty, equality and fraternity. These principles, understood in the manner of the French revolutionaries, were nothing but antecedents of communism. For this reason, they were severely condemned by Pope Pius VI in the Secret Consistory of June 17, 1793. In this he said, confirming the words of his encyclical *Inscrutabile Divinae Sapientiae*, of December 25, 1775:

"These accursed philosophers proceed to destroy the bonds of union among men, both those which unite them to their rulers, and those which urge them to their duty. They cry ad nauseam that man is born free and subject to the authority of no one, that society accordingly is a crowd of foolish men who stupidly yield to priests who deceive them and to kings who oppress them, so that the necessary concord between the priesthood and the civil power is only a monstrous conspiracy against the innate liberty of man [encyclical *Inscrutabile Divinae Sapientiae*].

"To the false and lying name of liberty these vaunted patrons of the human race add another deceitful name, equality; as though among men who have formed a civil society with so many diverse affections, uncertain inclinations, subject to the caprice of each, there was to arise no one to prevail by authority and power, who could constrain, moderate, and recall the wicked to the bounds of right. Without this, such a society, swayed by rash impetuosity and the clash of so many conflicting desires, falls into anarchy, and cannot escape a speedy dissolution: it is then with society as with harmony, when composed of the accord of various sounds. But if it has not, as a soul, a suitable accord of chords and voices, it produces only troubled noises and deafening dissonance" (Pius VI, *Pont. Max. Acta* [Rome: Typis S. Congreg. de Propaganda Fide, 1871], vol. 2, pp. 26-27).

* * *

These events not only shook Europe, but had harmful repercussion in the New World as well.

France at that time was mistress of the islands of Martinique, Guadeloupe, and Saint Domingue (present-day Haiti). These Caribbean possessions, until then prosperous and tranquil, deeply suffered the disturbances of the French Revolution. The slaves and the mestizos rose up against their masters and employers with the intention of shaking off their yoke, just as the nobility had been suppressed in the mother country.

Among the prosperous families of Saint Domingue was that of Jean Bérard du Pithon. Pierre Toussaint, a black, was one of his slaves.

Pierre was only 21 years old when the disturbances of the Revolution led the family to take refuge in New York. Toussaint accompanied them, and thence his story truly begins.

The family, belonging to the nobility, was able at first to live well in New York with the savings they brought with them. Like many of the French emigrants after the fall of the Bastille (1789) in Paris, who left the country with a fixed amount of money and the certainty that the Revolution would not last long, the Bérard du Pithon family also expected a quick return to their homeland, judging that the revolution in Saint Domingue would be short-lived. Many so deceived themselves and, depleting their financial resources, soon faced dire circumstances.

The Bérard family, then, had to reduce considerably the level of its social status, feeling threatened to resort to jobs incompatible with their condition in order to live.

It was in this sad predicament, after eleven years of happy association, that Monsieur Jean Bérard died in 1791, leaving the aristocratic Marie Elisabeth Bossard Roudanes a widow. She had to confront the adverse conditions alone and, moreover, in precarious health.

But the hand of Providence watched over her. The "hand of Providence": a beautiful metaphor to characterize the watchfulness with which God accompanies and aids the lives of His creatures. Religious art customarily presents it as a charitable white hand; in this concrete case, the "hand of Providence" was a black hand: the hand of Pierre Toussaint.

This modest slave, who could so easily have tried to escape from the yoke of his mistress in the United States, acted in relation to her with a dedication and a delicacy of sentiment that few children have even in relation to their own mother.

After completing a schedule of duties that required great selflessness and that he fulfilled to the end, Pierre Toussaint, by his own decision, strove even more in order that his mistress would not want for anything of the social conditions and comforts of life that corresponded to the education she had received.

At the suggestion of his deceased master, Pierre had learned the skills to practice the art of dressing ladies' hair in the small but already rich New York of that time. Imaginative and gifted with good taste, he developed various hairstyles that were much to the liking of his affluent clients, who then paid him well for his services. In a short time, Toussaint came to be sought out by all the rich ladies of New York, and he thus obtained the necessary resources to support his mistress.

However, he accomplished this with such skill and discretion that he was often able to hide from her a good part of his self-denial and generosity. He did this without lying, because

Toussaint was very truthful and, as a fervent Catholic, he avoided any transgression of the Commandments of the Law of God.

Very early in the morning, before beginning his work, Toussaint could be seen going to Saint Peter's Church on Barclay Street where every day for sixty years he attended Holy Mass (daily Communion becoming a custom of fervent Catholics only after the pontificate of Saint Pius X [1904-1914]) and prayed his rosary. Only after this did he begin his professional activities.

With the conditions created by Toussaint, Madame Bérard's shaken health slowly recovered and, with his encouragement, she could once again open her parlors to guests. Toussaint, having labored during the day as a hairdresser, worked gratuitously at night as a butler. Superbly dressed, with very gentle and pleasant manners, he served all his mistress's guests, and then delighted them with his violin, which he played excellently.

In time, a French refugee named Gabriel Nicolas, a skilled musician whose talent provided him a well-to-do life in New York, obtained the hand of the widow Bérard, who thus became Madame Nicolas. Although relieved for some time with the new marriage, misfortune returned to visit the noble lady. Due to the passing of an abstruse law, several New York theaters were closed and, with this, the main source of her husband's income disappeared. Toussaint's faithfulness was once again her support.

His work with the ladies of the high society of New York continued and he exercised a beneficent influence. During the work they talked about various subjects, and in everything he answered with so much correctness and made such wise commentaries that many regarded him as a counselor, asking his opinion about delicate personal problems. Some even went to his home when, surprised by some new problem, they urgently needed a judicious solution from Toussaint.

As one can imagine, Toussaint accumulated some savings. With this, he could have acquired his own freedom, but, ever a model in his self-denial, he preferred to remain in his condition as a slave and buy instead the freedom of his sister, who had come with him from Saint Domingue, and that of his future wife! Toussaint only acquired his own freedom much later, in 1807 at age 41.

In July of that year, shortly before dying, Madame Nicolas made it a point to grant Toussaint's freedom, in agreement with her husband.

In 1811, Toussaint married. Without ceasing to render services to Monsieur Nicolas as long as he remained in New York, Pierre established his own home. He was a model husband. The death of his wife in 1851, two years before his own, was a moral blow to Toussaint from which he never fully recovered. From then on his previously flourishing health began to deteriorate. This provides a measure of the richness of Toussaint's sentiments.

This richness of sentiments almost reaches the unimaginable. A part of the Bérard family had scattered in Europe with the French Revolution. Afterward, when the Terror ended and the emigrants began to return, Toussaint made efforts to know if these loved ones had survived and, if so, where and how.

What was his contentment when, through a French lady who passed through New York and whom Toussaint attended, he found out that Aurora Bérard, his old master's sister and his god-mother in Baptism, had not died as he had supposed but lived in Paris. She wrote her first letter to her godson as soon as she learned about him. Toussaint answered this letter and sent with it a dozen Madras handkerchiefs, highly esteemed by the French ladies of the time. Toussaint kept up a long correspondence with his godmother that ceased only with her death in 1834. One of her brothers, also living in France, was the object of Toussaint's epistolary watchfulness as well.

As one can see, a more exemplary dedication cannot be imagined.

But the life of all men is shaken by violent winds and these were not lacking in Toussaint's life. One was the brusque change in women's hairstyles, which became much more simple. His professional services became practically unnecessary to his affluent clients. This could have meant a complete ruin for Toussaint. However, being very skillful and able in everything, he did not let himself be discouraged. He adapted to the new styles and maintained his clientele, who now used his services more as a pretext for obtaining his daily visit and pleasant conversation.

*   *   *

These facts constitute a true epic of dedication of a Catholic soul to his family as well as to his masters. It is an epic accomplished in such a dedicated manner and with such brilliance that Toussaint's life reads like an innocent but highly attractive novel. Nevertheless, his life contains many more elements to properly attract our attention and serve as a theme for high reflections of a moral character. The reader will find all this by carefully reading and reflecting on this biography published by the Western Hemisphere Cultural Society.

We sincerely counsel you to do so.

A capital reflection, meanwhile, presents itself to our eyes. It is the fulgurant antithesis between Toussaint and the radical modern egalitarianism of which communism was a characteristic example. Having been born into the hard conditions of slavery and faced while still quite young by the flames of a social revolution full of incitement to revolt against his owners, Toussaint would have had easy means for freeing himself from this yoke. It would have been enough for him to have adhered to the revolutionary movement that a namesake of his, Toussaint L'Ouverture, successfully headed for a long time. Toussaint L'Ouverture was a little prefigure of the so-censurable Fidel Castro who has led a social and political revolution in Cuba to the last extremes. After thirty years of cruel dictatorship, Castro still holds the population of this island, formerly evangelized by the great Saint Anthony Mary Claret and deservedly called, due to its natural beauty, the Pearl of the Antilles, in misery and under the iron-grip of a true captivity.

While communism, on the one hand, is atheistic, Toussaint was the model of a believing and pious man. He adhered, as we have already said, to all of the Roman Catholic and Apostolic doctrine and fervently fulfilled the Commandments.

While the communist revolution is fundamentally egalitarian and preaches hatred against all superiors, Toussaint was the paradigm of a man with hierarchical spirit and love for his superiors, as the Fourth Commandment enjoins: "Honor thy father and thy mother." And while communism's cry of revolt could be perfectly condensed in Satan's exclamation of revolt, *"Non serviam,"* Toussaint's life, on the contrary, is summarized in this word that would be worthy of Saint Michael the Archangel: *"serviam."* He served. He served his family members; he served his masters; he served his clients; he served everyone to whom he could do good; and he did so with largess and generosity. The one he least served was himself. The ferocious egoism that Marx sought to incite in each one of his followers was precisely the contrary of the abnegated and generous spirit of Toussaint.

Thus, Toussaint seems to us as a man who, although of little learning, nevertheless understood the spirit of the Catholic Church so well that, in face of the phenomenon of social inequalities, he entirely accepted the doctrine of the Angelic Doctor, Saint Thomas Aquinas.

In very summarized form, this doctrine is that harmonious and judicious inequalities are not evil, but, on the contrary, are good. They are a condition of order on earth as in heaven. The great Doctor of the Church says that God, upon undertaking the creation of the universe, was necessarily moved by the intention of making the universe a reflection of His own perfections, but that, these perfections being multiple and infinite, there was not a single creature that could reflect them all at the same time. For this reason, He gave being to several creatures, each fitted with the duty of reflecting an aspect of His perfection.

Furthermore, the perfections have several degrees in creatures. It is through graduated perfections that creatures best reflect the absolute perfection, which is God.

This being so, men, in turn, and angels as well, were created unequal. This inequality is a condition for them to adequately reflect God.

Saint Thomas Aquinas thus affirms in the *Summa Theologica*:

"In natural things species are arranged in degrees; as the mixed things are more perfect than the elements, and plants than minerals, and animals than plants, and men than other animals; and in each of these one species is more perfect than others. Therefore, as the divine wisdom is the cause of the distinction of things for the sake of the perfection of the universe, so is it the cause of inequality. For the universe would not be perfect if only one grade of goodness were found in things" (*Summa Theologica*, I, q. 47, a. 2).

Thus, creatures are necessarily multiple. And not only multiple, but also necessarily unequal. This is the doctrine of the Holy Doctor:

"Furthermore, a plurality of goods is better than a single finite good, since they contain the latter and more besides. But all goodness possessed by creatures is finite, falling short of the infinite goodness of God. Hence, the universe of creatures is more perfect if there are many grades of things than if there were but one. Now it befits the supreme good to make what is best. It was therefore fitting that God should make many grades of creatures.

"Again, the good of the species is greater than the good of the individual, just as the formal exceeds that which is material. Hence, a multiplicity of species adds more to the goodness of the universe than a multiplicity of individuals in one species. It therefore pertains to the perfection of the universe that there be not only many individuals, but that there be also diverse species of things, and, consequently, diverse grades in things" (*Summa Contra Gentiles*, bk. 2, chap. 45).

Intrinsically, therefore, inequality is not an evil. It is a good. And absolute equality, on the contrary, is an evil. It was because they turned to this absolute equality that the rebellious angels rose up against God, when He revealed to them the Incarnation of the Word, and the superiority that Our Lord Jesus Christ would, therefore, have over them.

On the contrary, Saint Michael the Archangel, resisting Satan's cry of revolt, proclaimed the holiness and the perfection of a fundamentally unequal universe as is that of the angels.

This is a profound and admirable lesson for modern men, who, in their great majority, are so often imbued with the spirit of complete equality, even when not practicing it in their actions, and who so often revolt against those to whom they owe love, respect, and obedience: parents, teachers, employers, and others in positions of authority in the political, social, and economic spheres.

Well understood, this apologia of inequality does not include the praising of unjust inequalities. Regarding the rights inherent to human nature—those belonging to all men as men—all are equal, because all are men. But, to the extent that men are accidentally unequal, it is necessary to respect these inequalities, to love them and serve them. This is the great lesson we receive from Pierre Toussaint. We recommend all readers of this work to meditate on and imitate this lesson.

In America, where racial strife has so often brought lamentable discord and division, this grand example, who helps Catholics revere a black so worthy of all their respect and love, contributed to the eradication of mutual discord and distrust between the races and, thus, to the consolidation of concord among all Americans.

*   *   *

In short, Toussaint's life was a remote, but luminous, reflection, of the precept uttered by Saint Peter, who ordered the slaves of his time to obey their masters, not only when they are worthy of respect and affection like Madame Bérard, but even when they are harsh: "Servants, be subject to your masters with all fear, not only to the good and gentle, but also to the harsh" (1 Pet. 2:18).

PLINIO CORRÊA DE OLIVEIRA

PART ONE

THE records of distinguished characters are multiplied around us: the statesman who has toiled night and day for his country is held in grateful remembrance; the hero who has fought for the land of his home and people justly wins the laurels that are showered upon him; the scholar who devotes his pen to the instruction of his fellow-beings, the poet, and the historian gradually build for themselves monuments. But there is one class whose silent accumulation of good deeds is not computed, but which is daily increasing the amount of human happiness, and whose influence is like that of the crystal stream which wanders through the meadow, adding to its uncounted portion of wildflowers and verdure. Of such a one we would speak in the simple, unexaggerated language which corresponds to the subject of this memoir.

PIERRE TOUSSAINT was born in the island of St. Domingo [present-day Haiti], in the town of Saint Marc, on the Plantation de Latibonite, which belonged to Monsieur Bérard. The grandmother of Toussaint, Zenobe Julien, was a slave in the family, and selected as a wet-nurse for the oldest son. This maternal office she also performed for his sister.

It was customary in the West Indies for people of fortune to send their children abroad, to secure to them better influences than they could obtain on a plantation. Sometimes, at the age of four and five years, sons and daughters were separated from tender parents, with a degree of heroic sacrifice for which nothing but the importance of the measure could give their parents resolution.

Monsieur Bérard early decided to send his son to Paris to be educated; and to supply, as far as possible, the tenderness of a mother, Zenobe Julien was selected to accompany him, and to remain with him several months. This proof of the father's confidence in the bondwoman sufficiently demonstrates the reliance which both parents placed on her. When she returned to St. Domingo, it was to conduct the two daughters to Paris, who were to be placed at a boarding-school.

On leaving them there, she again returned to Saint Marc and resumed her attendance on her mistress. The parents so fully estimated the worth of this faithful domestic, that, as a reward for her fidelity and a proof of their entire confidence, they gave her her freedom. They knew well that her attachment to them formed the strongest bonds. John Bérard constantly wrote to her from Paris, sending her presents, and retaining his early affection.

Zenobe had a daughter whom she called Ursule. As the little girl increased in years, she became more and more useful to Madame Bérard, and was finally adopted as her waiting-maid and *femme de chambre*.

The subject of our memoir, Pierre Toussaint, was the son of Ursule, and became the pet of the plantation, winning all hearts by his playfulness and gentleness.

His grandmother, Zenobe, was particularly attached to him; yet when Monsieur and Madame Bérard concluded to rejoin their children in France, and called on Zenobe to accompany them, she did not hesitate for a moment, but gave them her *free* obedience, and cheerfully acceded to their wishes; for they no longer had the right to command. For the fifth time the faithful attendant crossed the ocean—a more adventurous and lengthened voyage than now—and after seeing her master and mistress settled in Paris, returned again to Saint Marc. Here she had the happiness of passing the evening of her life in the service of her nursling, John Bérard, who came back to reside on his father's plantation after he had completed his studies, leaving his two sisters with his parents.

Pierre Toussaint was born before the elder Bérard left the country, and Aurora, his youngest daughter, stood godmother to the infant slave. She was a mere child, and he could have no recollection of the ceremony; but as he grew older, he became more and more devoted to his little godmother, following her footsteps, gathering for her the choicest fruits and flowers, and weaving arbors of palms and magnolias. Toussaint's happiness was much increased by the birth of a sister, who was called Rosalie.

We can scarcely imagine a more beautiful family picture; it was a bond of trust and kindness. Slavery with them was but a name.

About the time of Pierre Toussaint's birth, 1766, and several years later, the island of St. Domingo, or Haiti, as it was usually called, was in its most flourishing state. The French colony was then at the height of its prosperity. The tide of improvement had swept over the land; forests had been cleared, marshes drained, bridges built over rivers, torrents converted into picturesque waterfalls. The harbors were made safe and commodious, so that large vessels could ride at anchor. Beautiful villas and cottages bordered the sea, while palaces and magnificent public buildings adorned the interior. Hospitals were built; fountains refreshed the air. Scarcely could imagination reach the luxury of this island, which seemed to contain in its bosom the choicest treasures of nature. Such an earthly paradise could not fail to attract foreigners. The French were proud of their colony, and it became a fashion with them to emigrate to the island. Some settled as planters, others passed to and fro at their pleasure, promoting commerce, goodwill, and the arts of refinement.

The terrible events which followed this flourishing era are too painful to record.

We go to the happiest period of Pierre Toussaint's life. John

Pierre Toussaint was born in 1766 in Saint Marc, Haiti, on the Plantation
de Latibonite, which belonged to Monsieur John Bérard du Pithon. During the period Toussaint lived there this French colony was known for its
variety of fruits and flowers, its palm and magnolia trees, its rich planta-
tions, its beautiful villas and cottages, its palaces and magnificent buildings.
The island was later shaken by the violent winds of the French Revolution,
at which time Toussaint moved to New York with the Bérard family.

Bérard successfully cultivated the plantation, treading in his
father's footsteps, and with patriarchal care exacting a due propor-
tion of labor, which he rewarded with kindness and protection.
Wealth flowed in upon him. He was tenderly attached to his
cousin, and finally married her. She had resided much on the
plantation, and partook of his attachment to the slaves, particularly to Zenobe and her descendants.

"I remember her," said Toussaint, "when the bridal took
place. She was very pale; her health was always delicate, but she
looked so lovely, and we were all so happy! and Rosalie and I
were never tired of gathering flowers for her, and we used to
dance and sing for her amusement." In one year after her marriage she began to droop. "Ah!" said Toussaint, "I can see her
as she lay upon the couch, panting for air—all so beautiful, out-
side and in; then Rosalie and I would stand at opposite corners
of the room and pull the strings of a magnificent fan of peacock's
feathers, swaying it to and fro, and we would laugh and be so
gay, that she would smile too; but she never grew strong—she
grew weaker."

She expressed a wish to go to Port-au-Prince—probably her
near relations resided there. She took Toussaint and Rosalie
with her.

About this time the troubles in St. Domingo began. The
revolutionary doctrines of France could not fail to influence
her colonies. Haiti looked at the contest for liberty and equality with the keenest interest. The wealthy proprietors joined
in the universal cry. But they had no idea of participating these
blessings with the free-born colored people; they still meant to
keep them in a subordinate state. A large number of wealthy
and intelligent merchants, but a shade or two darker than their
aristocratic brethren, stoutly contended for an equal share in
administering the affairs of the colony, and claimed their right
of representation, of sharing in the distribution of offices, and
all the immunities of free and independent citizens. This was
by no means the idea of the nobility of St. Domingo; and when
France subsequently espoused the cause of the mulatto free
population, and when the Abbé Grégoire spoke eloquently for

them in the National Assembly, the hatred of the whites knew no bounds. As yet only private attempts at annoyance had arisen on both sides; but a dark storm seemed threatening, for the disaffected had talked of offering their colony to the English. No fears were entertained of the slaves; they were considered as machines in the hands of their masters, and, without principles, wills, or opinions of their own, they were neither dreaded nor suspected; and so the contest seemed to be between the nobility and the free people of color.

Monsieur Bérard willingly consented to the change his young wife proposed in going to Port-au-Prince, hoping she might derive benefit from it. But no favorable symptoms occurred; her decline was rapid, and in one short month from her arrival she breathed her last, in her twenty-first year.

Toussaint and Rosalie returned to Latibonite at Saint Marc's. It was most touching to listen to Toussaint's description of his young mistress, as he saw her every day declining, yet then unconscious that he should soon see her no more!

The attachment of these two classes, of mistress and slave, might almost reconcile us to domestic slavery, if we only selected particular instances. But without suggesting whether there are few or many such, we may all understand the danger of institutions which leave to ignorant, passionate men the uncontrolled exercise of power. It is not, however, on the ground of individual treatment that the philanthropist, the statesman, and the moralist found their strongest arguments against slavery; it is on the eternal rights of man, on the immutable laws of God; and till it can be proved that the negro has no soul, we cannot plead for him merely on the score of humanity, or place him simply under that code of laws which, imperfectly it is true, protects the noble horse from abuse. It was for his divine right that Abbé Grégoire spoke so successfully.

We now arrive at what formed the great era of Pierre Toussaint's life. He had hitherto lived in the midst of luxury and splendor; for the apartments of Monsieur Bérard, as he describes them, were furnished in a style of expense that exceeded even modern prodigality. All the utensils of his mistress's chamber

were of silver lined with gold; the dinner service was of the same
metals. In St. Domingo, the tropical climate yielded its abun-
dant fruits, and the hardships of winter were never known.

Monsieur Bérard married a second wife, and still all was successful and prosperous. But this was not to last long. The troubles had now begun. He earnestly wished to preserve a neutral
position; but he found this impossible. His immense property
became involved; his perplexities increased in various ways; and
he determined to leave the island and repair to the United States
to pass a year, meaning to return when the storm was over and
tranquility restored. He took with him five servants, including
Toussaint and his sister Rosalie.

New York was their place of destination. Monsieur Bérard,
by the kindness of a friend, found a house ready furnished, of
which they took immediate possession. He brought sufficient
funds to enable them to live in good style for more than a year.
Madame Bérard also brought over her sisters, one of whom had
married General Dessource.

They formed at this time a merry and united family, with
plenty of society and amusement. "I remember," said a lady who
was well acquainted with them, "Toussaint among the slaves,
dressed in a red jacket, full of spirits and very fond of dancing
and music, and always devoted to his mistress, who was young,
gay, and planning future enjoyment."

All went on pleasantly with them for a year; but news from
the island grew more and more alarming, and Monsieur Bérard
thought it necessary to return to St. Domingo, to look after his
affairs. Previously to his going, he mentioned to Toussaint that
he wished him to learn the hairdressing business, and a Mr. Merchant, who dressed the hair of Madame Bérard, engaged to teach
him for fifty dollars. Monsieur Bérard, placing the property he
had brought over to this country in the hands of two respectable merchants, took leave of his wife, as he thought for a short
season. In the meantime, she remained tranquil and hopeful,
talking over her plans of living with Toussaint, telling him her
projects for the time to come, and concerting pleasant surprises
for her husband when he should arrive. She was much pleased

with Pierre's success as a coiffeur, and said how gratified Monsieur Bérard would be to find he had succeeded so well. Those who have known Toussaint in later years will easily comprehend the manner in which he was adopted into the confidence of his employers through life. His simple, modest deportment disarmed all reserve; he was frank, judicious, and unobtrusive. A highly cultivated and elegant woman said, "Some of the most pleasant hours I pass are in conversing with Toussaint while he is dressing my hair. I anticipate it as a daily recreation." The confidence placed in him by his master and mistress he considered a sacred trust.

Melancholy letters arrived from Monsieur Bérard. His property was irreclaimably lost; and he wrote that he must return, and make the most of what he had placed in New York. This letter was soon followed by another, announcing his sudden death by pleurisy.

Madame Bérard had not recovered from this terrible shock, when the failure of the firm in New York to whom her property was entrusted, left her destitute.

"Ah!" said Toussaint, "it was a sad period for my poor mistress; but she believed—we all believed—that she would recover her property in the West Indies. She was rich in her own right, as well as her husband's, and we said, 'O madam! you will have enough.'"

But this present state of depression was hard indeed to one who had always lived in luxury. The constant application for debts unpaid was most distressing to her; but she had no means of paying them, and she could only beg applicants to wait, assuring them that she should eventually have ample means.

Toussaint entered into all her feelings, and shared her perplexities; and though he had scarcely passed boyhood, he began a series of devoted services.

He was one day present when an old friend called on her, and presented an order for forty dollars, thinking her husband had left the money with her, and by no means divining her state of destitution. She assured him he should have the money, and requested him to wait a short time; she considered it peculiarly a debt of honor. When he went away, she said to Toussaint, "Take these jewels and dispose of them for the most you can get."

He took them with an aching heart, contrasting in his own mind her present situation with the affluence to which she had always been accustomed. He had by industry begun to make his own deposit; for, as a slave, he was entitled to make the most of certain portions of his time. In a few days he went to his mistress, and placed in her hands two packets, one containing forty dollars, the other her own valuable jewels, upon which the sum was to have been raised. We may imagine what were her feelings on this occasion!

At another time, the hairdresser of whom Toussaint had learnt his trade called on Madame Bérard for the stipulated sum. Toussaint heard her reply, with faltering voice, "It was not in her power to pay him; he must wait." Toussaint followed him out, and entered into an engagement to pay the sum himself, by installments, and at length received an acquittal, which he presented to his mistress. She was at first alarmed, and said, "O Toussaint, where can you have gotten all this money to pay my debts!" "I have got some customers, Madame," said he; "they are not very fashionable, but Mr. Merchant very good, he lets me have them; and besides, I have all the money that you give me, my New Year presents—I have saved it all." She was much surprised, and told him she did not know when she should be able to repay it. He told her it was all hers, that he never wanted that money again; that he had already good customers, and expected every day more and more. "My poor mistress," said Toussaint, "cry very much."

From this time he considered his earnings as belonging to Madame Bérard, except a small deduction, which he regularly set aside, since he had a purpose to execute which he communicated to no one. His industry was unceasing—every hour of the day was employed; when released, his first thought was his mistress, to hasten home and try to cheer her.

In this way he alleviated the burden of her troubles; his affectionate, loving heart sympathized in all her sorrows. His great object was to serve her. He was perfectly contented with his condition. Though surrounded in New York by free men of his own color, he said that he was born a slave—God had thus cast his lot, and there his duty lay.

Two of Madame Bérard's sisters died, and the family was thus broken up. A gentleman from Santo Domingo, Monsieur Nicolas, who had left the island about the same time with the Bérard family, cherished the hope, which many entertained for years, of recovering his property. In the meantime, like other unfortunate emigrants, he found himself obliged to convert those accomplishments which had made a part of his education to the means of living. For some time he performed as a musician in the orchestra of the theater, and gave lessons in music to a number of scholars. He was a constant friend of Madame Bérard, and they at length married. For some time they were sanguine in the hope of returning to the island, and taking possession of their property, but constant disappointment and perpetual frustration of her hopes wore upon Madame Nicolas's naturally delicate frame, and her health became much impaired. Monsieur Nicolas was a kind and tender husband, and did all in his power to alleviate her indisposition, and administer comfort to her.

Toussaint, in the meantime, was industriously pursuing his business as a hairdresser, and denying himself all but the neat apparel necessary for his occupation, never appropriating the smallest sum of his earnings to his own amusement, though at that season of youth which inclines the heart to gaiety and pleasure. Belonging to a race proverbially full of glee, and while on the island, among his sable brethren, first in the dance and song, he now scrupulously rejected all temptation for spending money, and devoted his time to his mistress. We have before alluded to the care with which he hoarded his gains. Besides the pleasure of surprising Madame with little delicacies, he had evidently another object in accumulating, of which he did not speak. He was successful, and took a respectable stand as a hairdresser. His earnings belonged in part to his mistress; but as she grew more sick, he delighted to add voluntarily the portion which belonged to himself. His sister Rosalie was a constant and faithful attendant, but Toussaint was both a companion and friend. Madame Nicolas had an affection of the throat, and was obliged to write rather than converse; to this faithful friend she used to express her wants on little scraps of paper, and he invariably supplied them, while she consoled herself with the idea that he would be fully indemnified eventually from her own property. He had no such belief; he wished for no return. In later years he said, "I only asked to make her comfortable, and I bless God that she never knew a want."

He strove to supply her with the luxuries of her tropical climate—grapes, oranges, lemons, and bananas; he regularly procured jellies and ice creams from the best confectioners, and every morning went to market to obtain what was necessary for her through the day. His business of hairdressing proved very lucrative, and kept him regularly employed. He attended one lady after another, in constant succession, and when released from his duties hastened to render new services to his invalid mistress. She felt that influence which a strong and virtuous mind imparts, and communicated to him her perplexities. He often read to her, and, adds one of his most cherished and faithful friends,* "Perhaps this scene, so touching to his feelings and elevating to his heart, in contemplating a being honored and beloved, gradually wasting away, may have been the foundation of that piety which has sustained him through life, and become deeply seated in his breast. He is a Catholic, full in the faith of his Church, liberal, enlightened, and always acting from the principle that God is our common Father, and mankind our brethren."

Toussaint seemed to understand the constitution of Madame Nicolas's mind; he reflected that she had always been accustomed to society, and that the excitement of it was necessary for her. "I knew her," he said, "full of life and gaiety, richly

---

* Mrs. Philip J. Schuyler, whose death took place in 1852, preceding Toussaint's about fifteen months. She was the daughter of Micajah Sawyer, M.D., of Newburyport, Massachusetts. To her notes the author of this memorial is principally indebted.

dressed, and entering into amusements with animation; now the scene was so changed, and it was so sad to me! Sometimes, when an invitation came, I would succeed in persuading her to accept it, and I would come in the evening to dress her hair; then I contrived a little surprise for her. When I had finished, I would present her the mirror, and say: 'Madame, see how you like it.' Oh, how pleased she was! I had placed in it some beautiful flower—perhaps a japonica, perhaps a rose, remarkable for its rare species, which I had purchased at a greenhouse, and concealed till the time arrived." Sometimes, when he saw her much depressed, he would persuade her to invite a few friends for the evening, and let him carry her invitations. When the evening arrived, he was there, dressed in the most neat and proper manner, to attend upon the company; and he was sure to surprise her by adding to her frugal entertainment ice cream and cakes. It appeared his great study to shield her from despondency—to supply as far as possible those objects of taste to which she had been accustomed. In this constant and uniform system, there was something far beyond the devotion of an affectionate slave; it seemed to partake of a knowledge of the human mind, an intuitive perception of the wants of the soul, which arose from his own finely organized nature. In endeavoring to procure for her little offerings of taste to which she had been accustomed, he was unwearied: not because they had any specific value for himself, but simply for the pleasure they gave to her. All he could spare from his necessary wants, and from the sum which he was endeavoring to accumulate, and to which we have before alluded, was devoted to his mistress. "Yet one rule," he said, "I made to myself, and I have never departed from it through life—that of not incurring a debt, and scrupulously paying *on the spot* for everything I purchased."

But not all this affectionate solicitude, nor the cares of a kind husband, for such was Monsieur Nicolas, could stay the approach of death. Her strength rapidly declined, and every day Toussaint perceived a change. At length she was confined to her bed. One day she said to him, "My dear Toussaint, I thank you for all you have done for me; I cannot reward you, but

God will." He replied, "O Madame! I have only done my duty."
"You have done much more," she said; "you have been everything to me. There is no earthly remuneration for such services."

A few days before her death, she called Toussaint to her
bedside, and giving him her miniature, told him she must execute a paper that would secure to him his freedom. Monsieur
Nicolas, who was present, said, "Save yourself this exertion—
everything you wish shall be done." She shook her head, and
replied, "It must be done *now*."

Her nurse from infancy, Marie Bouquement, had accompanied her mistress to New York. She was aunt to Toussaint. Free
papers were given to this faithful domestic by Madame Bérard
and her sisters in St. Domingo, in which we find this sentence:
"We give her her freedom in recompense for the attachment
she has shown us, since the troubles which afflict St. Domingo,
and release her from all service due to us."

This woman, whom she tenderly loved, she committed to
Toussaint's care in a most touching manner. "As you love my
memory," she said, "never forsake her; if you should ever leave
the country, let her go with you."

The deed was legally executed which secured to Toussaint his
freedom, and which she had strength to sign. She then desired
him to bring a priest, made her confession, received her last Communion, and died at the age of thirty-two.

She was a most gentle, affectionate woman, and deeply attached to those around her. We think a letter of hers, addressed
to her negro nurse, will not be uninteresting in this connection. It appears that Marie, after seeing her mistress safely settled in New York, returned again to see her family, as among
Toussaint's papers the following letter is found from Madame
Nicolas:

"New York

"How, my dear Marie! is this the way you keep your prom-
ise? You told me you would write to me as soon as you reached
the Cape. Everyone has written, but I find no little note from
you. Have you forgotten me, my dear Memin? This thought

makes me too sad. I was sorry to part with you, but I would not tell you all I felt, lest you should have changed your mind, and passed the cold winter here. So now you are at the Cape.

"I hear you reached there after a voyage of thirty days. Were you ill, my dear Memin? How are you now? I am impatient to hear from you. Tell me news of your children. If it had not been for this last news, we should by this time have been at the Cape; as soon as the French troops arrive, we shall return. If you are not well off, come back to me, and we will all go to St. Domingo together. You know that you are a second mother to me; you have filled the place of one. I shall never forget all you have done for my poor sisters, and if efforts could have saved anyone, I should now have them all. But God has so ordered it, and His will be done! Ah, dear Memin, your religion will support you under all your sufferings—never abandon it!

"Adieu! Write me soon, or I shall think you do not love me any longer.

"I am, always, as you used to call me, your
"BONTÉ."

The little fancy names of endearment were peculiar to the West Indian mistresses and slaves. Marie Bouquement returned again to New York.

PART TWO

AFTER the death of Madame Nicolas, Toussaint remained with her husband. Monsieur Nicolas lived on the first floor of a house, with one servant, who was his cook; and Toussaint continued to go to market for him, and to perform many gratuitous services. In this manner they resided together for four years, on Reed Street.

Marie Bouquement also had a room on the same floor of the house, and supported herself by her industry.

Rosalie, who was still a slave, was engaged to be married, and Toussaint at once put into execution the project he had long contemplated, and for which he had been accumulating the needful money by degrees. This was the purchase of his sister's freedom. Of his own freedom he never seems to have thought, but it was all-important to him that Rosalie should enter life under the same advantages as her husband and those around her. With a delicacy for which he was always remarkable, he never mentioned this subject to Madame Nicolas, though we cannot but think that she would at once have bestowed it without price. Probably the subject never occurred to her.

Toussaint paid his sister's ransom, and she was soon married. He had now time to think of himself. He had formed an attachment for Juliette Noel, and they were married in 1811, and

35

continued to live in the same house with Monsieur Nicolas, having two rooms in the third story.

At the end of four years Monsieur Nicolas left New York for the South, and a constant interchange of letters and kind offices on Toussaint's part took place, continuing till the death of Monsieur Nicolas. The following extract from a letter of Monsieur Nicolas to Toussaint, written long after, will show how highly this gentleman respected and appreciated him:

"July, 1829

"I have received your letter, my dear Toussaint, and share very deeply the sorrow which the loss of your niece must bring upon you. No one knows better than I, how much you were attached to her; however, as you say very truly, we must resign ourselves to the will of God. I am sorry to hear that Juliette has been ill, and hope that your next letter will speak of her reestablished health. I have not written to you for a long time, my dear Toussaint—not that I do not think of you, or that I love you less, but I was troubled because I was not able to send you anything; however, I know your heart, and feel quite sure you will not impute this delay to want of inclination. You have no idea how unhappy I am when I cannot meet little debts. But, my dear Toussaint, I fail every day; I am at least ten years older than when I last saw you. Both courage and strength begin to fail, and add to all this, that I do not hear a word from France about our claims. You can understand my sad situation; but a few years longer will put an end to my misery. However, I do not despair to see you again before I pay the debt to Nature. In the meantime think of me, write to me, and be assured that you will always find me your true friend,

"G. NICOLAS"

A period of prosperity seemed now to have dawned on the faithful Toussaint. He was happy in his conjugal connection. Juliette was of a merry, cheerful disposition and fully estimated the worth of her husband. Indeed, how could it be otherwise? She saw him universally respected, and treated as a friend by everyone. As a hairdresser for ladies, he was unrivalled: he was the fashionable coiffeur of the day; he had all the custom and patronage of the French families in New York. Many of the most distinguished ladies of the city employed him; we might mention not a few who treated him as a particular friend.

A pleasant novel, said to be written by a Southern lady, but published in New York, *The Echoes of a Belle*, gives a graphic description of Toussaint as a hairdresser: "He entered with his good tempered face, small earrings, and white teeth, a snowy apron attached to his shoulders and enveloping his tall figure."

He went continually from house to house performing the office of hairdresser, and was considered quite as a friend among the fair ladies who employed him. They talked to him of their affairs, and felt the most perfect reliance upon his prudence; and well they might, for never in this large circle was he known to give cause for an unpleasant remark. Once a lady, whose curiosity was stronger than her sense of propriety, closely urged him to make some communication about another person's affairs. "Do tell me, Toussaint," she said, "I am sure you know all about it." "Madam," he replied with dignity, though with the utmost respect, "Toussaint dresses hair, he no news journal."

At another time he was requested to carry a disagreeable message. He immediately answered, "I have no memory."

Toussaint had delayed his marriage with Juliette, till he saw his sister Rosalie, as he believed, well settled in life, and mistress of her own freedom; but all his affectionate endeavors could not secure to her the happiness he had so fondly anticipated.

In 1815 Rosalie had a daughter born, but her prospects had been cruelly frustrated; her husband proved idle and dissipated, and Toussaint almost entirely supported her. The little infant was named Euphemia by her uncle, but the mother's health rapidly declined. Dr. Berger was her able and humane physician; he pronounced her in a decline. Juliette took home the infant of six months old, and brought her up by hand. Very soon the mother was removed to Toussaint's roof, and, after lingering a few months, breathed her last. Previously to this event, Marie Bouquement had died, carefully watched over by

Toussaint, who considered her as a legacy bequeathed to him by his mistress.

Euphemia was a sickly, feeble child. Dr. Berger did not give much encouragement that she would live; but Toussaint, who was always sanguine, fully believed that her life would be granted to them. Both his and Juliette's assiduity was unremitting for her; no parents could have done more. Every day Toussaint took the feeble little creature in his arms, and carried her to the Park, to the Battery, to every airy and pleasant spot where the fresh breezes sent invigorating influence, hoping to strengthen her frame and enable her lungs to gain a freer respiration. The first year of her life was one of constant struggle for existence, but God blessed their untiring efforts, and the frail plant took root and flourished.

An incident occurred in Toussaint's life about this time, which deeply interested him. He was summoned to the City Hotel to dress the hair of a French lady, who was a stranger. She could speak no English, and therefore was very glad to converse with him in her native language. She spoke to him of her lonely feelings, and of her painful separation from a dear friend, who was now in Paris. Toussaint told her there were many agreeable French families in New York. "Yes," she said, "she had letters to a number, but no one could take the place of her Aurora Bérard."

It was the first time he had heard his godmother's name mentioned for many years. Could it be *her* of whom the lady spoke? A few inquiries settled the matter; it was indeed the same—she who in the happy period of his infancy had stood sponsor at the baptismal font, who had sometimes visited his dreams, but of whose very existence he was doubtful. How many touching recollections arose to his mind! Again the palmy groves of his beautiful native isle were before him; again he was gathering fruits and flowers for his little godmother, and performing a thousand antic sports for her amusement. But such delusions are momentary; he was once more Toussaint the hairdresser, and hastened back to communicate this delightful surprise to his faithful Juliette. The lady was soon to leave the city and return to Paris; he wrote to Aurora by her, but from some unfortunate mistake, when he carried his letter she had sailed.

His disappointment was great, but in three months afterwards he received the following letter from Aurora, saying she had heard of him through her friend, and expressing her affection for his grandmother and mother, and her kind interest in him.

"À MONSIEUR TOUSSAINT, *Coiffeur**
"Paris, November 27, 1815

"Madame Brochet, on her return to this city, fifteen days since, has given me news of you, my dear godson. I, as well as my brothers and sisters, am truly grateful for the zeal that you manifested in wishing to learn something of us, and for the attachment which you still feel for us all. After the information that Madame Brochet gave me, I cannot doubt that you will be glad to receive a letter from me. I write to you with pleasure, and I have felt much in learning that you are prosperous in your affairs, and very happy. As to us, my dear Toussaint, we have never left Paris. Our situation is not happy. The Revolution deprived us of all our property. My father was one of the victims of that frightful period. After being confined six weeks in prison, and under constant inspection of the government, on their own place, near Paris, both he and my mother died of grief. My brothers and sisters are married, but I am not, and am obliged to make exertions to live which have impaired my health, which is now very poor. Were it not for that, I might be tempted to accomplish the voyage you desire; but I am not the less sensible to the offers you make me, through Madame Brochet, and I thank you sincerely. It is consoling to me to know, amidst all my troubles, that there exists one being who is so much attached to me as you are. I wish we could live in the same town, that I might give you details by word of mouth about my family. [Here follows a short account of her brothers and sisters and their children.]

---

* It is but justice to observe, that all the original letters in this volume addressed to Toussaint are translations from the French.

"Write to me, my dear Toussaint, about your wife; I know you have no children. Do you know anything relating to St. Domingo? What has become of all our possessions, and our ancient servants? Tell me all you know about them. Have you any of your former companions in your city? My nurse Madelaine and your mother, are they still living? Tell me everything you know. Adieu, my dear godson. Do not forget to write to me, and depend upon the affection of your godmother, who has never forgotten you, and who loves you more than ever, since she finds you have always preserved your attachment to
"AURORA BÉRARD"

This letter Toussaint immediately answered, and accompanied it by a dozen Madras handkerchiefs. The French ladies highly prized this article, for at that time they were considered a most tasteful and fashionable headdress. Juliette always wore them, and was often asked to teach ladies to fold them, and give them the graceful and picturesque air which she gave to her own. From this time letters were frequently exchanged between Aurora and her affectionate godson. He sent her Canton crape dresses, and other articles which were of great price in France, and all of the best quality. These presents she gratefully acknowledged, but there is a very natural fear expressed that he has sent too expensive ones. In alluding to the crape dresses, she writes: "To judge from the dearness of the articles here, I fear you may have made some sacrifice to purchase them, and this idea gives me pain."

Soon after the letter sent by Aurora, Toussaint received the following from Monsieur Bérard, the brother of Aurora:

"Paris, 1815
"I have learned with pleasure and gratitude, my dear Toussaint, all that you have done for my brother Bérard and his widow, and the attachment you still entertain for our family. Since I have known all this, I have wished to write to you, and express the love and esteem I feel for you. It is from Mesdames D__, R__, and C__, I have received these details. I was so young when I left St. Domingo, that I should certainly not recognize

your features, but I am sure my heart would acknowledge you at once, so much am I touched with your noble conduct. All my family share these feelings, but more particularly my sister Aurora. I do not despair of returning to St. Domingo, and of finding you there, or in the United States, if I take that route.

"Adieu, my dear Toussaint. Give me news of yourself, and believe in my sincere friendship.

"BÉRARD DU PITHON"

This renewal of his early intercourse with the Bérard family was a source of great happiness to Toussaint. We regret that none of his letters to his godmother remain; but hers sufficiently prove the affection on both sides. He even proposed removing to Paris with Juliette, and consults her on the eligibility of such a step. Her answer, an extract from which is here given, is most kind, considerate, and disinterested. His wish is evidently to support her, as he had his mistress, by his own industry.

"Paris, December 1, 1818

"I have seen Mr. S___ today. This gentleman appears to be much attached to you, which gives me great pleasure. We talked together of your wish to come to France. If I only consulted my own desire to see you, I should say, come at once; but your happiness my dear godson, is what I think of above all things, and since everyone from New York tells me that you are happy, highly esteemed, and much beloved by most respectable persons there, would you be as well off here? Those who know your resources better than I can, may advise you with more confidence. If I were rich, this would be of little consequence. I should call you near to me, for I should be too happy to have a person to whom I could give all my confidence, and of whose attachment I should feel certain. This would be too desirable for me, not to ask you to come; but my position is a sad one. I could not be useful to you, and I fear you would not be so happy as you deserve. I speak to you like a mother, for be assured that your godmother would be most happy to see you. Although I have not seen you since my childhood, I love you like a second mother, and I can never forget the services you have rendered to my brother and his wife. My brothers and sisters share these feelings, and we never speak of you without emotion."

The following is from another letter of Mademoiselle Bérard, of a little later date:

"Your friends have not left me ignorant of all the good you do, and that you are the support of the colored women of our plantation. You must induce them to work, for you should not give away all your earnings. You must think of yourself, of your wife, and niece, whom you look upon as a daughter. I hear that Hortense is with you; she belonged to me, and must be young enough to work and support herself. You will do her a service if you induce her to work; tell her so from me. It gives me pain to find that you are still without news of your family; here we know nothing. Let us trust in Providence. Your feelings of piety make me believe that God is also your consolation; you are right, and the assurance that everyone expresses of your religious character gives me great pleasure. I feel deeply, my dear godson, all that you tell me of your desire to see me, and to serve me. I understand your noble feelings. Your attachment adds much to my happiness, for there are so few persons in the world who resemble you, that I appreciate you as you deserve."

This pleasant intercourse continued for many years. At length the following letter came:

"July 28, 1834

"You are already in sorrow, my dear Toussaint, and the sad news I must announce to you will only augment it. Two months have passed since your beloved godmother was taken from us by sudden death. My heart is so deeply oppressed by this affliction, that I can scarcely write. A few days before her death she spoke of you; she wished to write to you, being very anxious at not having heard from you for a long time. What pleasure she would have experienced in receiving your last letter, which arrived about fifteen days since! The news I send to you will be sad, but you may be assured of the affection that every

PIERRE TOUSSAINT

1766–1853

PRAYER

Lord God, source of love and compassion, we praise and honor You for the virtuous and charitable life of our brother in Christ, Pierre Toussaint.

Inspired by the example of Our Lord Jesus, Pierre worshipped You with love and served Your people with generosity. He attended Mass daily and responded to the practical and spiritual needs of friends and strangers, of the rich and the poor, the sick and the homeless of 19th century New York.

If it is Your will, let the name of Pierre Toussaint be officially raised to the rank of Saint, so that the world may know this Haitian New Yorker who refused to hate or be selfish, but instead lived to the full the commandments of heaven and the divine law of love — love for God and for neighbor.

By following his example and asking for his prayers, may we too be counted among the blessed in heaven.

We ask for this through Christ our Lord, Amen.

Imprimatur: Most Reverend Patrick J. Sheridan, D.D., V.G.

PIERRE TOUSSAINT GUILD
1011 First Avenue, Room 1316 · New York, N.Y. 10022

member of our family feels for you, and myself in particular. My dear Toussaint, it will be a great pleasure to hear from you. I hope that Divine Providence will mitigate the painful remembrance of your adopted niece. Man can offer only words, but God, who sends the affliction, can diffuse into our souls all necessary fortitude. May you have recourse to the throne of grace, and that blessed future life where all our thoughts ought to center. I hope that your dear godmother now enjoys perfect happiness; since the death of our parents she has suffered much. Indeed, for several years she has experienced the pain of rheumatism in frequent attacks; her patience and resignation to the will of God, and her entire confidence in the Mother of God, will be her propitiation. I love to think that God is good; He knows our hearts, and will judge us."

The letter closes with assurances of the love and gratitude of all the family. It is from Madame de Berty, the sister of Aurora Bérard.

Toussaint's situation was now prosperous in every way; he lived in a pleasant and commodious house, which was arranged with an air of neatness, and even gentility. Juliette was merry and cheerful; she loved her little parties and reunions; they had wealth enough for their own enjoyment, and to impart to those who were in need. They were conscientious Catholics; charity was for them, not only a religious duty, but a spontaneous feeling of the heart. One instance may here be mentioned of the quiet, silent manner in which they bestowed their good deeds. A French gentleman, whom Toussaint had known in affluence, a *white man*, was reduced to poverty; he was sick and suffering, craving a delicacy of food which he had no means to procure. For several months Toussaint and Juliette sent his dinner, nicely cooked, in such a way that he could not suspect from whom it came. "If he had known," said Toussaint, "he might not have liked it; he might have been proud." "Yes," said Juliette, "when Toussaint called to see him sometimes, he would say, 'Oh, I am well known! I have good friends; every day somebody sends me a nice dinner, cooked by a French cook'; and then perhaps he would enumerate the different viands. My good husband would come home, and tell me, and we would laugh very much."

When Euphemia was about seven years of age, a friend of Toussaint's proposed her being taught music. Her uncle was wholly opposed to the idea; he thought it would involve much expenditure of time and money, and he saw no advantage to be derived from it. He said the little girl had her own sweet voice, and sang like the birds, yet they were not taught music.

Some time after, a warm and true friend of Toussaint's, who knew his worth, urged him to let her give lessons to Euphemia in music; this was the lovely and amiable Miss Cesarine Meetz.* She persevered in going to his house, with her notes in her hand. Finally he consented, on her suggesting that it might hereafter become a means of support to his niece. This representation, with her gratuitous instruction, obviated his objections; but then another arose. So tenderly guarded was the little Euphemia, that he never suffered her to go into the streets alone, and he felt that his time could not be spared to attend her. Miss Meetz, in her benevolent zeal, beautiful and young as she was, offered to come herself and give the lessons. But Toussaint's never failing sense of propriety would not allow of this arrangement; and Juliette, her good aunt, accompanied her three times a week to her kind young friend, to receive her lesson. This was continued for four years. Toussaint purchased a piano, and she made all the progress that could be expected.

It was obvious, however, that her religious and moral cultivation was the first object with her uncle; his tenderness and judgment were constantly blending their efforts for the improvement of her heart and mind. He was most desirous to make her a being who would be capable of fulfilling her duty toward her Creator and her fellow-beings. No household instruction was omitted. Juliette was an excellent housekeeper, and the little girl was her aunt's assistant. They were constantly inculcating lessons of charity with her pleasures.

Toussaint was much interested in the Catholic Orphan School

---

* Later Mrs. Moulton, who resided in Paris.

for white children. "On Euphemia's saint's day," he said, "I always took her with me to the cake shop, and we filled a large basket with buns, jumbles, and gingerbread, which we carried to the Orphan Asylum." I said to him, "You let her give them to the children?" "Oh no, madam! that would not be proper for the little black girl. I tell her, ask one of the sisters if she will give them to the children. When they were sent for, Euphemia stood on one side with me to see them come in, and when they received the cake they were so glad, and my Euphemia was so happy! One day as we went there, she asked me, 'Uncle, what are orphans?' I answered, they are poor little children that have no father or mother. For a moment she looked very sad; then she brightened up and said, 'But have they no uncle?' O madam! I feel so much, so much then, I thank God with all my heart."

He had the happy art of making everyone love him, by his affectionate and gentle manner. His deportment to his wife was worthy of imitation even by white men. She was twenty years younger that he was, and no doubt had a will of her own; but she always yielded it to Toussaint's, because she said she *was not obliged to do it.* A friend related to me an amusing scene she witnessed. Juliette was about to purchase a mourning shawl, for she had just lost a relative. The shawls were exhibited. "How do you like this for mourning?" she said to Toussaint. "Very pretty," he replied. "I think," she said, "it is handsome enough for church." "Oh yes! very good for that." "Don't you think it will do to wear if it rains?" "Oh, certainly!" "I think it will do sometimes to wear to market, don't you?" "Very nice," he replied; "pray take it, Juliette; it is good for mourning, for church, for rain, and for market; it is a very nice shawl." Juliette secured it, much satisfied with her bargain.

Since I began this memoir, I have learned that Toussaint purchased Juliette's freedom before he married her. To this circumstance he did not allude in the history of his early life; probably from the sense of delicacy for which he was so remarkable. He went immediately after the ceremony to the City Hall to have the papers ratified.

Euphemia was taught reading, writing, and all pursuits adapted to her age. When she was five or six years old, she was a most engaging child; her manners were strikingly gentle, her countenance and expression pleasant, and her behavior excellent, modelled upon her uncle's ideas of obedience and deference, which he had always practiced himself. He often contrived to throw in a word of admonition to the children around him; to one little girl where he visited he said, "Miss Regina, your mother very good; obey her now, you will be happy when you are older." This lesson years after she gratefully mentioned.

How devotedly he loved his little niece, many will yet remember. She seemed fully to understand his affection, and clung to him as the vine clings to its support. She was delicately formed, and her figure slight; he would put his arm around her, and say, "My Euphemia," with a tenderness that was affecting; there appeared something sacred in his love, as if he felt that God had entrusted her to his protection, and, by depriving her of all other earthly support, had made him responsible for her future welfare.

When she was about twelve years old, Toussaint procured her a French teacher. French was his own and his wife's language, of course that of his family; but he wished her to speak it grammatically. He also let apartments in his house to a respectable white woman, a widow, who taught Euphemia English, and who after a while collected a small school of young children.

It was a striking trait in his character, that everything in which he engaged was thoroughly done; there was a completeness in his plans, and their execution, which commanded confidence, and which perhaps was one of the causes of the respect which he inspired. This sometimes led ladies to say, that Toussaint "was a finished gentleman." His moral qualities, however, gave him this distinction; for with the most perfect modesty he knew exactly what was due to others and to himself, while his heart overflowed with that Christian kindness which far surpasses mere worldly politeness. He was observant of all the forms of the Roman Catholic Church; through winter and summer he missed no matin prayers, but his heart was never narrowed by

This miniature of Toussaint, made in his late fifties, shows his remarkable vitality. This vitality served him until late in his life, when even in his old age he was seen working his way to distant parts of New York City on errands of charity. His moral qualities, formed by his deep Catholic faith, shine in his face.

any feeling as to sect or color. He never felt degraded by being a black man, or even a slave; for he considered himself as much the object of Divine protection as any other human being. He understood the responsibility, the greatness, of the part allotted him; that he was to serve God and his fellowmen, and so fulfill the duties of the situation in which he was placed. There was something truly noble and great in the view that he took of his own nature and responsibility. No failure on the part of the master could in his opinion absolve a slave from his duty. His own path was marked out; he considered it a straight one and easy to follow, and he followed it through life. He was born and brought up in St. Domingo at a period which can never return. In the large circle around him there were no speculations upon freedom or human liberty, and on those subjects his mind appears to have been perfectly at rest. When he resided in New York, he still preserved the same tranquil, contented state of mind, yet that he considered emancipation a blessing, he proved, by gradually accumulating a sum sufficient to purchase his sister's freedom. It was not his own ransom for which he toiled, but Rosalie's, as has been previously said, for he wished that she might take her station as a matron among the free women of New York. But he does not appear to have entertained any inordinate desire for his own freedom. He was fulfilling his duty in the situation in which his Heavenly Father chose to place him, and that idea gave him peace and serenity. When his mistress on her deathbed presented him his liberty, he most gratefully received it; and we fully believe he would not have suffered any earthly power to wrest it from him.

There are many in the present day who will view this state of mind as degrading, who consider the slave absolved, by his great primary wrong of bondage, from all obligation to the slaveholder. Not such was Toussaint's idea. He did not ask, like Darwin's African slave, "Am I not a man and a brother?" but he felt that he *was* a man and a brother. It was the high conception of his own nature, as derived from eternal justice, that made him serene and self-possessed. He was deeply impressed with the character of Christ; he heard a sermon from Dr. Channing, which he often quoted: "My friends," said Channing, "Jesus can give you nothing so precious as Himself, as his own mind. May this mind be in you. Do not think that any faith in Him can do you good, if you do not try to be pure and true like Him." We trust many will recognize the teachings of the Savior in Toussaint's character.

Madame Toussaint loved Euphemia with the same affection that she would have bestowed on her own children, had she possessed any. She was an excellent wife, and respected her husband's feelings in all things. She was cheerful and good-humored, had a most pleasant, cordial laugh, and a ladylike deportment. Her figure and features were fully developed, and much more African than Toussaint's, though she was several shades lighter. Their house was the abode of hospitality, and many *pale faces* visited them.

At the age of fourteen, Euphemia seemed to have attained firmness and strength, and we can hardly imagine more domestic happiness, or a picture of more innocent enjoyment, than Toussaint's household afforded. His peculiar devotedness and tenderness toward Euphemia seemed to be richly rewarded. He had no idea of making her a being that would be incapable of fulfilling the daily avocations of life. She was carefully taught all domestic duties; it was her great pleasure to aid her aunt, and she was never happier than when she was allowed to assist in the work of the family. When she grew old enough to make her uncle's coffee, it would be difficult to say which received most pleasure, the uncle or the niece, the first time she brought it to him, and said, "I made it all myself."

Toussaint's friends knew well they could afford him no higher gratification than by bestowing kind attentions upon this child of his adoption and darling of his heart. Many and constant were the little presents she received. Toys, dolls, and bonbons were the early gifts; afterwards books, and those things suitable to her increasing years. He always spoke of the kindness and solicitude of his beloved friend, Mrs. Peter Cruger, originally Miss Church, for his Euphemia, with a gratitude that could hardly be expressed. He had another devoted friend, to whom his heart was bound by the strongest ties of reverence and affection—the one to whom we have before alluded. One has long since passed away, the other but yet a little while was with us. They both loved and cherished the little girl for her uncle's sake, and she seemed to be daily fulfilling his fond wishes.

She was carefully educated in the forms of the Catholic Church, and no lesson of love, charity, or kindness was forgotten, that might soften and penetrate her youthful heart. What delight to Toussaint to return to his happy home after the fatigues of the day, and meet this young creature of his affections, who enlivened him with her music, cheered him by her smiles, and interested him by relating all her little pursuits since they had separated! Perhaps she would repeat to him some story she had read during his absence, and she would say, "It is a true story, I read it in a book."

Her exercises in writing were very regular; every week two little notes in French and English were handed to Toussaint from his niece. We have many of them before us; we insert a few, which are about equal to those of white children at her age.

"New York, February 23, 1827

"DEAR UNCLE,

"Oh, how sorry I am that you were not there to see Miss Meetz married; she looked so sweet and beautiful; she looked like an angel; but what I think was so good in her, that she should come and kiss my aunt and me, before all the company. I believe nobody would do it but her. It will come quite difficult to me to call her Mrs. Moulton. I have made one mistake already.

"Adieu, Dear Uncle,
"EUPHEMIA TOUSSAINT."

"DEAR UNCLE,

"What bad weather we have now! I hope it will not last long, for it is very disagreeable for you, who have to run all over the town, and everywhere; but God knows better than we do; He does everything for the best, and it is so singular that we cannot be contented. Dear uncle, I will be very much obliged to you if you will give me one shilling to buy cotton to finish my frock; now I have begun it I want to finish it very much, and after that I want to embroider a vandyke. I have not seen Mrs. Cruger a long time; I wish to see her very much.

> "Adieu, Dear Uncle,
> "EUPHEMIA TOUSSAINT."

"DEAR UNCLE,

"Oh, I must write to Mrs. Moulton to tell her about your having your miniature taken;* I know that it will please her, and make her laugh. I have several things to tell her that will please her very much. Dear uncle will you excuse me for writing so short a letter this week, for I composed it in a great hurry.

> "Your EUPHEMIA TOUSSAINT."

The little girl's attachment to this kind friend, Mrs. Moulton, was unceasing through her short life. She often complained of the difficulty of calling her by her married name, and said, the other was much more natural.

It is with grief we see dark clouds gathering over this smiling prospect. The health of Euphemia began to decline, and she was threatened with consumptive complaints. Juliette mentioned her fears to her uncle; he could not believe it, he could not listen to it. But alas! it soon became too evident that the disorder of the mother had sown its hereditary seeds. Then there was no rest for poor Toussaint night or day. He required the unremitting consolations of his friends to soothe and calm his mind. He hung over the darling of his affections with an intensity of feeling which seemed to threaten his own life.

The good Father Powers devoted himself to uncle and niece. It was judged best not to acquaint Euphemia with her situation. It was her delight to rest in her uncle's arms, to tell him how she loved him, and what she would do for him when she got well.

Sometimes when friends called, they would find him seated on her bed, where she lay supported by pillows, her presents

---

* The miniature alluded to is the one from which the lithograph has been taken.

strewn around her, for people were untiring in sending her little gifts to interest and amuse her. Her uncle would hand her the articles that lay beyond her reach, and amuse her by recounting her treasures. So many more good things were sent her than she could even taste, that she said playfully, "I make uncle eat all these up, but I keep the flowers to look at."

Toussaint felt deeply the proofs of friendship which were daily accumulated in attentions to his darling, and often expressed his unworthiness in the humblest manner, saying, "I thank God for all His goodness."

It was a great consolation to him that Euphemia suffered but little. She gradually wasted away, without any painful struggles. He said one day, "God is good; we know that here on earth, but my Euphemia will know it first there," pointing upwards.

A few months brought the rapid decline to a close; and the loved one who had been so carefully cherished and guarded, and whose slumbers had been watched over from infancy, slept the last sleep of death.

> "And what is early death, but sleep
> O'er which the angels vigils keep;
> Around the white-robed seraphs stand,
> To bear the young to the spirit-land."

For a long while Toussaint could only say to those who came to comfort him, "My poor Euphemia is gone"; and as his lips uttered these words, he covered his face with his hands. He grew thin, avoided society, and refused to be comforted. But his mind was too pious and too rational to indulge long this excess of sorrow. He listened to high and holy consolations, and found resignation in the prayers of his Church. Those who witnessed his struggles to command himself at this time, and perform his daily duties, have spoken of him with reverence.

Toussaint received a most consolatory letter from his friend, Mrs. Cruger, who was then in France, soon after the death of his niece. We give the following translation:

when He was
63

"1829

"I need not say, my dear Toussaint, how much I sympathize with you; my heart and my soul follow you in your last cares for this cherished child, to whom you have ever been the best, the most tender of fathers. My tears have flowed with yours; but I could not weep for *her*, I wept for *you*. When we resign to the Eternal Father a child as pure as the heaven to which she returns, we ought not to weep that an angel has entered into a state of happiness which our feeble conceptions cannot picture, and you, my good Toussaint, who are piety itself, will realize this consoling thought, the only one you can now welcome in this severe affliction. The life of Euphemia has been almost a miracle; she owes her existence to your constant care and watchfulness. Her short life has been full of happiness; she has never known the loss of a mother; far happier than hundreds of others raised in the wealthiest and most elevated classes, the most gentle virtues and affections have surrounded her from her cradle, and she has been taken from a paradise on earth to enter into an eternity of happiness. Could you have secured the future to her? If death had struck you instead of her, to what dangers might she not have been exposed! May the consciousness of the duty you have so faithfully discharged mitigate this bitter sorrow. You have given back to a cherished sister the child of your adoption, before either sin or sorrow had touched her, and they will both wait for you in that mansion reserved for beings as excellent and virtuous as you are."

The effect of Euphemia's death, and the deep affliction it caused Toussaint, seemed eventually to produce a more energetic purpose of usefulness; his earnest desire was to benefit others. To accomplish this object, when funds were wanting, he would use his influence in promoting fairs, and, in individual cases, raffles; disposing of elegant and superfluous articles at a just price, when their owners were reduced by poverty.

His ingenuity in contriving means of assistance to others was remarkable. A French lady, who was much embarrassed in her circumstances by the depreciation of her small property and the failure of her rents, consulted Toussaint on the possibility of doing something for her support. He suggested her teaching French. She said very frankly, that she was inadequate to it, that she had no grammatical knowledge. "Madam," he said, "I am no judge, but I have frequently heard it said that you speak remarkably pure and correct French." This was really the case, for she had been educated in the best society. "That is a very different thing," she replied, "from teaching a language."

Toussaint, after some moments of reflection, said, "Should you be willing to give lessons for conversing in French?" She replied that she should be quite willing.

He at once set about procuring scholars among his English friends, many of whom appreciated the advantage of free and familiar, and at the same time correct conversation, for their children; and thus pupils were not wanting for the lady, and she was able to support her family by these simple means till the sudden rise of her rents relieved her from her embarrassment. This method was quite an original idea of Toussaint's at that time, though it has since been adopted even in our own language.

On occasion of some fair for a charitable purpose, Toussaint would go round to his rich friends and represent the object, and they placed so much confidence in his judgment, that they would often add trifles to swell the list, and always take a number of tickets; and in this way he was able to collect considerable sums for the benefit of the orphan and the widow.

It must not be supposed that Toussaint's charity consisted merely in bestowing money; he felt the moral greatness of doing good, of giving counsel to the weak and courage to the timid, of reclaiming the vicious, and, above all, of comforting the sick and the sorrowful. One of his friends said that "his pity for the suffering seemed to partake of the character of the Savior's tenderness at the tomb of Lazarus." When he visited his friends in sorrow, his words were few; he felt too deeply to express by language his sympathy. Once he said, "I have been to see poor Madam C__." (She had met with a most heavy bereavement.) "And what did you say to her?" said a friend. "Nothing," he replied, "I could only take her hand and weep

with her, and then I went away; there was nothing to be said."
He felt that, in the first moment of stunning grief, God alone
could speak to her.

When he entered the house of mourning, an air of sympathy
pervaded his whole manner, the few words he uttered were those
of faith and love, and he was often successful in communicating
comfort to the sorrowful.

We must not omit his wonderful capacity in sickness; how
often he smoothed the pillow and administered relief to disease.
He was constantly summoned as a watcher, and gave his services to the poor without money or price. At a time when the
yellow fever prevailed, and the alarm was so great that many
were deserted, Toussaint discovered that a man was left wholly
alone. He was a stranger, but he took him to his house, nursed
him, watched over him, and restored him to health. This stranger
was a white man!

Like others, he sometimes met with ingratitude for his services; in one particular instance he persevered through difficulties
and discouragements in endeavoring to serve a French family,
and succeeded in procuring situations for two of the young men;
but as they grew successful, they rather avoided their benefac-
tor. "I am glad," said Toussaint, "they so well off; they want
nothing more of me."

Because Pierre Toussaint was an unlettered man, many people who were surprised at his character, and at his numberless
good deeds, attributed his excellence wholly to his natural disposition. They said, "He has the best *instincts*—he was born
good." Those who knew him better saw that he was governed
by a high and noble principle. In a world of passion and error
it is idle to talk of human instincts as securities of virtue. Toussaint reflected deeply; he had no theories of philosophy; he would
not have understood much of the sentimental language with
which our novels abound; but, as we have before seen, he understood the plain teachings of Christianity. He often quoted,
in his native language, from the Sermon on the Mount, and the
beatitudes seemed to have found their way to his heart. His whole
life was one of thought and observation; he had a surprising

insight into character, and a wonderful tact in classing his friends. To some, even where he was sincerely attached, he was never communicative, for he knew they were not judicious; to others, with whom he had daily intercourse, he was careful not to commit himself, for he knew they were not sincere; but there were others to whom he gave his whole heart, as though he truly believed them but little lower than the angels.

When we speak of Toussaint's friends, we do not include his own people of color, though most gladly would we procure their testimony were it in our power. That he was a fast and true friend to them we know, but our walks have not led us among them; yet by this noble specimen we are induced to believe what they may become by treading in his footsteps. The friends we mean to particularize were those to whose houses he daily resorted—people in New York of the highest class in rank, cultivation, and wealth. It was by such he was sought and honored, and long after his labors as hairdresser had diminished, by the simpler fashion of the times he was requested by them to continue his daily visits. His profession began with the age of powder and pomatum, when immense fabrics were reared upon the female head; and to have an idea of these, the young must go back to ancient pictures, where they will see them in all their glory. When powder was relinquished, still the style of hairdressing was somewhat architectural. During the French Revolution perukes or wigs were introduced, and of course adopted by our American ladies. These seemed to furnish the strongest proofs of the caprice of fashion, as it was generally found that those on whom nature had liberally bestowed black hair went through the process of the razor, and appeared with flaxen or light brown wigs; so, in reverse, the blonde belles astonished their admirers by appearing with glossy raven curls. Of course there could be no attempt at deception in this matter; it was one of the caprices of fashion which had its reign and passed away.

Through all these changes Toussaint continued to be the favorite, and was summoned to shave the beautiful heads he had so often dressed, and prepare them for the modern wig. Then

again the perukes were discarded, and the natural hair suffered
to grow, and what were called crops succeeded, with the short
hair curled over the head. Still Pierre stood in high favor; no
curls were so beautifully arranged as his. As the hair began to
recover its growth, the Grecian fashion was adopted—the hair
fastened on the back of the head and falling in curls like those
of the sculptured Venus. Still Toussaint was all-important, and
ready to adopt any fashion his employers chose; but he looked
on with the eye of a philosopher. "Fashion keep change, change,"
said he; "all good, the way poor people live."

A lady told me that one day, when he came to pay his daily
visit, they were preparing dresses for a wedding. "I well remember," she said, "the thoughtful manner with which he stood looking at the flowers, laces, and gay silks strewn about the room.
I said, 'Why do you look so grave, Toussaint?' 'O madam,' he
said, 'I go to a great many places; I go into one house and they
cry, cry, cry—somebody dead. I go into another, and it is all
laugh, laugh—they are happy and glad. I go to another, it is all
shut up dark, they move very softly, they speak in a whisper—
somebody very sick. I come here, it is all dance and sing, and
flowers and wedding dresses. I say nothing; but it makes me think
a great deal.' "

Although always received with gladness and respect by the
heads of the house, his humility, good sense, and kind feeling
made him equally welcome to the domestics. He was often consulted by them, and when he entered the house, he generally
exchanged a few words; he excited in them no envy or ill-will,
which it might have been expected would arise, from seeing a
colored man treated with so much more distinction than themselves. The truth was, that they respected him, they felt the value of his good opinion, of his recommendation, and, above all,
they confided in the kindness of his heart.

This was in truth his great characteristic, the goodness of his
heart. "The heart will live forever. Of mere ingenuity, learning, and ability, much must fail us on the floor of heaven, left
behind with the world it knows of, and to perish with it." But
the heart will live on, not only hereafter, but here. Obedience

This photograph was taken toward the end of Pierre Toussaint's long life of dedication and self-denial. His countenance and bearing mirror his self-control, refinement of feeling, good judgment, and keen perception.

and resignation toward God, faith in the future, patience and commiseration for the sick and suffering, and love toward those of your own household, and to those around you, are not perishable in their nature; their influence is felt on all who come in contact. And thus it was with Toussaint; his heart was not only kind and affectionate, but merry and cheerful; it was filled with trust and confidence, and gave him the happy power of dispelling gloom and anxiety in others. Perhaps few reflected on the subject, yet they all felt that they loved to see him throughout the household.

On New Year's day he was always among those who came to tender their good wishes; every house from the drawing room to the kitchen was open to him, and every hand extended. We presume few remember him in his early manhood. Then he was tall and well made, and with the flexibility of limb which belongs to his race. He was truly an African, not as we see him in a degenerate form, but as Mungo Park describes him in his travels through Western Africa. "Every evening when the sun goes down, all Africa is alive with dance and song. The sound of music, rude though it be, stirs the leaves of the palm-tree from the marts of Ophir to the coast of Congo." Toussaint's lively description of these evenings on his native plantation reminds us of the traveler's account. Some of the songs of the West Indian negroes are yet preserved among us, and are remarkable for their childlike expression of human nature. The specimen which Park gives of an African song must be familiar to us all: "The poor white man, faint and weary, came and sat under our tree," etc.

The death of Toussaint's most dear and beloved friend, Mrs. Cruger, was a heavy affliction to him as well as to others. We insert a letter addressed to him on that occasion, from a French lady:

"Havre, 1840

"I am very sorry to learn the death of your truly estimable friend, Mrs. Cruger. The good Archbishop of Bordeaux, Bishop Chevereux, said to me, 'We are left on earth to weep for our friends.' We must believe that her good deeds and her virtues will find favor in the sight of the God of mercy, whose precepts she has followed all her life.

"Adieu, my dear Toussaint! Although we may not meet again in this land of exile, yet I trust we shall be reunited in our true country, heaven. Let us live so as to merit this happiness."

PART THREE

THE period in Toussaint's life which occurred from the time of Euphemia's death for a succession of years seems to have been an uncommonly tranquil one. His union with Juliette was happy. She was the daughter of a respectable woman named Claudine Gaston, who came to this country as a nurse, as has been before mentioned, with a French family, by whom she was much beloved. She was a judicious and an affectionate wife, by her neatness and order making his house pleasant to him, and taking a more than equal share in the labors of the family.

Every man must value the respect of his wife, and Toussaint could not but be gratified with the evident delight Juliette received from the attentions paid him. When her friends congratulated her on having such a good husband, her frank, happy smile, displaying rows of white teeth, gave a full assent to their commendations.

Toussaint said of himself, that he possessed a quick temper, that he was born with it, and was obliged to bear it about with him. We doubt not that it was true, because he had a lively sensibility to everything; yet to those who knew his self-command and forbearance, this trait made him the more interesting. One of his intimate friends, in alluding to his confessions

61

and penitence on the subject, said: "I never heard him speak ill of anyone; if he could say no good, he was silent. Even those who were ungrateful to him met with no angry rebuke; it seemed to be his object to forget all injuries."

Toussaint had a quick sense of the ridiculous, and like most of his race, when he was young, was an excellent mimic; as he grew older he relinquished this power, so amusing to others, as a dangerous one. He played on the violin for small dancing parties at one time, and taught one or two boys to play on this instrument, saying, if they did not derive profit from it, it would at least be an innocent amusement.

One of the methods in which Toussaint did essential good was by bringing up colored boys one after another, sending them to school, and, after they were old enough, teaching them some useful business. In all these plans of charity Juliette united.

The neatness and order of their household was striking. Toussaint purchased a pleasant and commodious house on Franklin Street, and a gentleman of the highest respectability took rooms there for some months. From a note of his I have permission to make extracts:

"I am sorry to hear that Toussaint is on his death-bed, though I do not believe he has cared much about living since he lost his wife. Such was the even tenor of his way while I lived under his roof, that nothing occurs particularly to my memory. You know there is no being on earth who presents so few prominent and recollectable points as a 'perfect gentleman.' If you undertake to describe any such person whom you have ever known, you will find him the most indescribable. So it was with Toussaint. His manners were gentle and courtly; how can this simple statement be expanded into details, so as to give a better idea of them? The most unaffected good humor at all times, the most respectful and polite demeanor without the slightest tincture of servility, the most natural and artless conversation—all this I remember of him, as everyone else remembers who knows him; but all his intercourse was so unobtrusive that it is difficult for me to recall anything marked. I remember how much I was pleased with his deportment and behavior toward his wife.

Juliette was a good woman, but unlike Toussaint; she was flesh and blood, while he was possessed of the spirit of one man out of many thousands. I never met with any other of his race who made me forget his color. Toussaint, for his deportment, discretion, good sense, and entire trustworthiness and fidelity, might have discharged creditably all the functions of a courtier or privy councillor. His politeness, which was uniform, never led you for a moment to suspect his sincerity; it was the natural overflow, the inevitable expression of his heart, and you no more thought of distrusting it than of failing to reciprocate it, and I cannot imagine that anyone could offer him an indignity."

Such is the testimony of a gentleman thoroughly acquainted with the world. I remember Juliette's opening a drawer and saying, "This is Mr.___'s linen, I have all the care of it"; and it certainly did her the greatest credit.

We have no authority to say much of Toussaint's views of slavery; in that, as in all things else, he *acted* rather than *theorized*. As we have seen, his earnings, all that he did not spend on the comfort of his mistress, were carefully hoarded for his sister's freedom, and his wife's freedom he purchased before he married her. We cannot doubt how highly he prized liberty for the slave, yet he was never willing to talk on the subject. He seemed to fully comprehend the difficulty of emancipation, and once, when a lady asked him if he was an Abolitionist, he shuddered, and replied, *"Madame, ils n'ont jamais vu couler le sang comme moi."* "They have never seen blood flow as I have"; and then he added, "They don't know what they are doing."

When Toussaint first came to this country, the free negroes and some of the Quakers tried to persuade him to leave his mistress. They told him that a man's freedom was his own right. "Mine," said he, "belongs to my mistress."

When the colored people in New York celebrated their release from bondage, on July 5, 1800, they came to Toussaint to offer him a prominent part in the procession. He thanked them with his customary politeness, congratulated them on the great event of emancipation, but declined the honor they assigned him, saying, "I do not owe my freedom to the State, but to my mistress."

There are so many instances of his devotion to the sick that we do not particularize them; but one lady mentions, that when the yellow fever prevailed in New York, by degrees Maiden Lane was almost wholly deserted, and almost every house in it closed. One poor woman, prostrated by the terrible disorder, remained there with little or no attendance; till Toussaint day by day came through the lonely street, crossed the barricades, entered the deserted house where she lay, and performed the nameless offices of a nurse, fearlessly exposing himself to the contagion.

At another time he found a poor priest in a garret, sick of the ship-fever, and destitute of everything. He made his case known, procured him wine and money, and finally removed him to his own house, where he and Juliette attended upon him till he recovered.

A friend once said to him, "Toussaint, you are richer than anyone I know; you have more than you want, why not stop working now?" He answered, "Madam, I have enough for myself, but if I stop work, I have not enough for others."

By the great fire of 1835, Toussaint lost by his investments in insurance companies. Some of his friends, who knew of his slow, industrious earnings, and his unceasing charities, thought it but just to get up a subscription to repair his losses. As soon as it was mentioned to him he stopped it, saying he was not in need of it, and he would not take what many others required much more than he did.

Among the numerous letters which Toussaint received, there are many from foreign parts. Persons of rank and high consideration wrote to him for years.

In 1840 Toussaint received the following letter from a friend at Port-au-Prince:

"MY DEAR TOUSSAINT,

"You will receive this by the Abbé __, who has left this country because he could not exercise his functions as a priest of God ought to be able to do. His holy duties are shackled by laws which subject him every moment to judges, who, according to the rules of our faith, are not competent to direct a priest in his duties as a minister of God. For reasons like these, he leaves this country; but he can inform you on this subject better than I can."

This gentleman was received by Toussaint with much respect and cordiality. He left New York very shortly, and a few months after, a letter, from which we make the following extracts, reached Toussaint:

"Rome, 1841

"MY VERY DEAR FRIEND,

"You are no doubt surprised not to have heard from me since I left New York, but I can assure you this omission has not arisen from forgetfulness of you or your dear wife. On the contrary, I have thought of you constantly, but my engagements have prevented my writing until now.

"On my arrival in this city, I was presented to the Propaganda, and was received by his Eminence Cardinal Fransoni with much attention and kindness. I was offered other missions, but I preferred and received permission to continue my studies at Rome for two years in the College of the Twelve Apostles, and the Propaganda pays all the expense during my residence in Rome. Today for the first time I put on the Roman ecclesiastical habit. I have received permission from the Cardinal Vicar-General of the Pope, to celebrate the Holy Mass in all the churches of Rome. There are, I believe, four hundred, some of them the largest and finest in the world; indeed they are little heavens upon earth, adorned with everything which can be procured in gold, silver, hangings of silk and satin, in marble statuary, in paintings, and mosaics. I wish I could give you a more minute account. Present my respects to the Rev. Mr. Powers, and believe me that I hold you and your kind wife in constant remembrance. With my best wishes for your temporal and eternal welfare, permit me to subscribe myself.

"Your very sincere friend."

We add a few extracts of letters from his own race. The following is from Constantin Boyer:

"Port-au-Prince, 1836

"MY DEAR FRIEND,

"I begin by wishing you a happy new year, as well as to madam, your wife. However, it is only wishing you a continuation of your Christian philosophy, for it is that which makes your true happiness. I do not understand how anyone can have a moment's peace in this world if he does not have constant reference to God and His holy will."

Another colored friend in Port-au-Prince writes as follows:

"1837

"You wish me prosperity, dear friend; what can touch my heart more than to receive your benedictions—the benedictions of a religious man. I have known many men and observed them closely, but I have never seen one that deserved as you do the name of a religious man. I have always followed your counsels, but now more than ever, for there are few like you. Good men are as rare as a fine day in America."

The following is from a colored woman to Madame Toussaint:

"Port-au-Prince, 1844

"This is the second letter I have written to you without waiting for an answer; but the gratitude I owe to you, my very dear friend, and to your husband, induces me to write, every good opportunity. After the services and the kindness you have shown me, during my residence in New York, I hope I never shall forget you. Since our arrival here, we have been in constant trouble and anxiety; the country is not tranquil. I fear that we shall be obliged to return to Jamaica again. At the other end of the coast, more than twelve hundred persons have gone to Jamaica. We are in a country where you can get no one to serve you or to help you. They all tell you they are free, and they will serve no one."

The following extract is from a letter by a colored friend:

"Port-au-Prince, 1838

"Let us now speak of politics. I have the honor to send you the treaty between France and Haiti, that you may see the conditions of agreement between the two powers. If I were to give you all the details, I should have to write a journal. But you will have them before your eyes. I can tell you, however, that since the arrival of Baron de Lascase there has been nothing but fêtes, dinners, breakfasts, and balls, in the city and the environs. The company consisted of the captains of frigates, the French Consul and his staff, generals, colonels, and other officers of Haiti. Would you believe that great numbers of persons wished to give them breakfasts, and could not? These gentlemen were always engaged by one or another. Le Baron de Lascase gave a ball to the Haitian ladies; never has anything like it been seen in Port-au-Prince. The company was the captains of frigates and brigs, as well as their officers. Ah! it was a splendid ball. They left, the 22d of March, with two Haitian missionaries, who have gone to France to get a receipt for the money which has been given, and to see to the ratification of the treaty.

"The Chamber of Representatives is open since the 10th of April. I hope they will lower the duties, and that will give us a more open commerce, and be a great advantage to us. The President made a fine discourse at the opening of the Chamber, but I could not get it to send it to you. It will come by the next opportunity. I assure you that the Baron de Lascase has been very much pleased with the Haitian gentlemen. They left Port-au-Prince with regret, after having made such pleasant acquaintances. May God keep you, Sir, in His holy keeping! It is not we who will see the happiness of this country, but our children will. If they behave themselves well, they will enjoy the happiness which has been denied to their ancestors."

The following is extracted from another letter of Constantin Boyer:

"Port-au-Prince, June 13, 1842

"My dear friend, do you know (unhappy country!) that there exists no longer Cape Haitien, nor Santiago, nor Port-au-Paix! These three cities were destroyed, on the 7th of May last, by an earthquake. While I speak of it, my hair stands on end. Never has living soul seen such a terrible earthquake. Santiago, such a pretty city, so well built, all with walls like the Cape, all houses of two or three stories high, all has been thrown down in half a second. At the Cape not a house stands upright. The trembling lasted for five minutes, rapidly, with great force. At Gonaive the earth opened, and a clear stream of water rushed out. At the same time a fire broke out and consumed twenty houses. At Port-au-Paix the sea rose violently nearly five feet, and carried off the rest of the houses which had not fallen. At the Cape six thousand persons have been killed under the ruins, and two thousand wounded. At St. Domingo all the houses have not fallen; they are, however, nearly all shattered and uninhabitable. The shock was much more violent towards the north than at the south; but this gives you some idea of what has taken place in this poor country. It happened at half past five in the evening. This country is now most miserable."

The following is from a young colored man:

"Saint Thomas, 1849

"My dear and venerable Compatriot,

"So far off as I am from you, I think of you always. I wend my way to Franklin Street at least once a day, in imagination, and the recollections of Boston or Lowell, of New York or Jersey City, never leave me. Yes the *Union* is a beautiful thing (*belle chose*), and the United States is a beautiful country. It offers something much more beautiful than other countries. It is its love of order, of work, its industry, that makes it first among the nations. They are surprised in the Colonies at the enthusiasm with which I speak of the United States, because in general the men of our race here suppose that all people of color are treated like cattle there. I wish I could tell you something satisfactory of our country; but this gratification is a long way off. If there is not bloodshed, there are deceptions, iniquities, the same bad tendencies—terror is the order of the day."

The following is an extract from a letter from an old friend of Toussaint's. It may be interesting from its touch of humor.

"Chicago

"MY DEAR OLD COMPANION,

"I am glad to hear that your horrible winter has neither killed you nor given you any serious illness. Thanks to your regular habits and your fervent prayers, you are still in good health, and I hear very prosperous. But you are still a negro. You may indeed change your condition, but you cannot change your complexion; you will always remain black. Do they mistake you for a white man, that you have a passport everywhere? No; it is because you perceive and follow the naked truth. Many think that a black skin prevents us from seeing and understanding good from evil. What fools! I have conversed with you at night when it was dark, and I have forgot that you were not white. The next morning when I saw you, I said to myself, Is this the black man I heard talk last night? Courage! Let them think as they please. Continue to learn, since one may learn always, and communicate your wisdom and experience to those who need it. I must now write to you about the ladies here. They are great coquettes, go with their heads well dressed, which they arrange themselves with great taste. Your business (hairdressing) would be worth nothing here. You must not come to this place to make your fortune; it would be a bad speculation."

We feel as if we had hardly done justice to the constant and elevated view which Toussaint took of his responsibility toward his own race. He never forgot that his color separated him from white men, and always spoke of himself as a negro. He sometimes related little anecdotes arising from this circumstance which amused him. One occurs to me that made him laugh heartily. A little girl, the child of a lady whom he often visited, came and stood before him, looking him steadily in the face, and said, "Toussaint, do you live in a black house?"

When he was very sick, a friend who was with him asked him if she should close a window, the light of which shone full in his face. "*O non, Madame,*" he replied, "*car alors je serai trop noir*"; "Oh no, madam, for then I shall be too black." This humorous notice of his color, without the slightest want of self-respect, was entirely in keeping with his character. He was a true negro, such as God had made him, and he never strove to be anything else. The black men represented as heroes in works of fiction often lose their identity, and cease to interest us as representatives of their race, for they are white men in all but color. It was a striking trait in Toussaint, that he wished to ennoble his brethren, by making them feel their moral responsibility as colored men, not as aping the customs, habits, and conversation of white men. He never forgot that he "lived in a *black house,*" nor wished others to forget it.

For many years Toussaint's life seems to have passed unmarked by any sorrows which do not occur to everyone. He had accumulated what to his moderate views was an independence, and enabled him to assist others. Juliette's mother lived with them, and was supported by him till she died. He had no connections of his own, but his kindness to all who needed it was unceasing. We think there are many who will recollect this period, and the cheerful little parlor where they convened their guest.

One of their social parties was pleasantly described to me by a white American acquaintance who had called on them, and whom Juliette invited with a companion to visit her. They belonged to the household of one of his most cherished and respected friends. They found only two Frenchwomen as guests besides themselves. The table was most neatly and handsomely set out, with snowy damask tablecloth and napkins, and exhibiting many of the elegant little memorials pertaining to the tea-table which had been sent them as presents from their friends in Paris. Juliette sat at the head, and waited on them, treating them with her delicious French chocolate, but of which she did not herself partake. When they had finished the repast, they

Toussaint wrote many letters in his great concern for others. Shown above is part of a letter, in his own hand, to his friend William Schuyler.

went into the contiguous room, and Toussaint joined the party. It was thus his sense of propriety led him to draw the line. He never mingled the two races. This might have been in some measure the result of early teaching, but there was evidently a self-respect in avoiding what he knew was unwelcome.

We find a letter of Toussaint to Juliette, which we insert:

"I have this moment received your letter, my dear wife, and I answer it on the spot. Everything goes on well here. I have a great wish to see you, but I wish much more that you should remain as long as you are pleased to do so, for I love my wife for herself, not for myself. If you are amused at Baltimore, I hope you will remain some days longer with your good friends. I thank them for having received you so kindly. Present my compliments to Miss Fanny, and tell her that I hope she will not set you too many bad examples. I know that, though she is very devout, she is *un peu méchante* [a bit naughty]. I hope you will bring away with you her devotion, but not her *méchanceté* [naughtiness]."

There was often something sportive and paternal in Toussaint's manner towards his wife, and when the difference in their ages was understood, it was easily accounted for. He had ransomed her when she was fifteen, and when he was himself in his thirty-seventh year. They were most truly attached to each other. *"Je ne donnerois pas ma Juliette,"* he said to one of his French friends, *"pour toutes les dames du monde; elle est belle à mes yeux,"*—"I would not give my Juliette for all the women in the world; she is beautiful in my eyes."

Both of them enjoyed excellent health, and probably Toussaint never supposed he should be the survivor. It was otherwise ordered. Juliette's health began to fail, and some alarming symptoms appeared. As in Euphemia's case, he was sanguine that she would recover. He said, "She is much younger than myself. She is strong, very strong. She is nervous; she will soon be better." But it became evident that she grew more ill, and he could no longer shut his eyes upon her danger.

"I often went to see Juliette," said a friend to me. "Between her chamber and her husband's there was a small room, which was fitted up with a crucifix, a prie-dieu, and many beautiful emblems of the Catholic faith, gifts to Toussaint, which he carefully treasured. 'Ah,' she said, 'he prays for me there; it is all the comfort he has; he will soon be alone. Poor Toussaint!' "

When her death came, it was a dreadful blow to him. He never recovered from the shock. It seemed to him most strange that she should go first, and he be left alone; yet he constantly said, "It is the will of God." Soon after her death, his own health became impaired. The strong man grew feeble; his step slow and languid. We all saw that Toussaint was changed. Yet he lingered on, daily visiting beloved friends who sympathized in his great loss, and still continuing his works of beneficence.

We have adverted to the gaiety and playfulness of Toussaint. They often met answering sympathies among his friends. We extract one or two passages from the letters of a lady who was travelling in Europe, and who well understood these traits in his character:

"1849

"I have returned from church. The service was performed in a Catholic chapel, with all the insignia. I thought of my dear Toussaint, and send my love to him. Tell him I think of him very often, and never go to one of the churches of his faith without remembering my own St. Pierre, and nobody has a better saint. I am glad to hear from him and his good Juliette."

We add a short note from the same lady:

"DEAR TOUSSAINT,

"I go to the Catholic churches all over; they are grand and ancient. I always remember my own St. Pierre, and often kneel and pray with my whole heart. Ah, dear Toussaint, God is everywhere! I see Him in your Church, in mine, in the broad waste and the full city. May we meet in peace and joy. Ever and ever.

"Your true friend."

We find among Toussaint's papers continual proof of his charitable gifts and loans, and of his efforts to discover any of his own family who might yet remain in St. Domingo, and also of the family of his aunt, Marie Bouquement. In his will he set aside four hundred dollars to be paid to her descendants in case they could be found within two years.

His health was now evidently failing, yet morning after morning, through snow and ice and wintry frosts, his slow and tottering step was seen on his way to Mass, which he never once failed to attend for sixty years, until a few months before his death; and later in the day, his aged frame, bowed with years, was to be seen painfully working its way to a distant part of the city, on errands of love and charity. A friend said to him thoughtlessly, "Toussaint, do get into an omnibus." He replied, with perfect good humor, "I cannot, they will not let me."

One bitter pang remained for him; to watch by the death-bed of that being who, from her exalted station, had poured strength and consolation into his wounded heart; who had often left the gay circles of fashion to speak to him words of peace and kindness, and who, when the shadows of death were coming over her, gave orders that Toussaint should always be admitted. Many were the fervent and silent prayers that the aged man breathed by the side of her bed, with clasped hands and closed lips.

Toussaint was a devoted disciple of his Church; her books of instruction were his daily food, his prayer-book was always in his pocket, and the maxims of Thomas à Kempis were frequently introduced in his serious conversation. His illustrations were often striking. In speaking to a Protestant friend of the worship of the Virgin, he said, turning to a portrait of a near relation of hers in the room, "You like to look at this: it makes you think of her, love her more; try to do what she likes you to do." In this interesting manner he described his own feelings toward the pictures and images of the Virgin Mary.

As he grew more feeble he was obliged to give up his attendance on the church. This occasioned him some depression. One of his Protestant friends who observed it said, "Shall I ask

a priest to come and see you? Perhaps you wish to confess."
After a long pause he said, "A priest is but a man; when I am
at confession, I confess to God; when I stand up, I see a man
before me."

His simple method of expressing his convictions was striking, and often instructive. He was enlightened in his own faith,
not from reading, but from a quick perception of the truth.

A lady who had known Toussaint from her childhood wrote
a letter when she heard of his illness, from which the following
passages are quoted:

"If my mother were living, how much she could tell us of
Toussaint! But unfortunately I never kept notes of the many
incidents she used to relate of his character; I regret it sincerely
now. At the time of Euphemia's death we were in France, but
most deeply did we feel for him.

"When we returned I saw him constantly, and began to comprehend him, which I never did fully before. I saw how uncom-
mon, how noble, was his character. It is the *whole* which strikes
me when thinking of him; his perfect Christian benevolence,
displaying itself not alone in words, but in daily deeds; his entire faith, love, and charity; his remarkable tact, and refinement
of feeling; his just appreciation of those around him; his perfect
good taste in dress and furniture; he did not like anything gaudy,
and understood the relative fitness of things. He entertained an
utter aversion to all vain pride and assumption. He spoke of a
lady he had known in poverty who was suddenly raised to
wealth. She urged him to call and see her. He was struck with
the evident display of her riches. She talked to him of her house,
her furniture, her equipages, her jewels, her dresses; she displayed
her visiting cards with fashionable names. To all this Toussaint
silently listened. 'Well,' she said, 'how do you like my estab-
lishment?' 'O madam!' he said, 'does all this make you very
happy?' She did not answer; she was not happy, poor woman!
She was *poor in spirit*; she never knew the pleasure of making
others happy.

"I recollect how invariably he consulted the dignity of others,
as well as his own. A lady was staying with me, and being a

Saint Peter's Church in New York City, on the square recently dedicated to Pierre Toussaint. This church replaced the old Saint Peter's Church, where Toussaint faithfully attended daily Mass for over sixty years.

Roman Catholic, she wished to go to Saint Peter's Church, and
asked Toussaint for a seat in his pew, on Sunday morning. He
said, 'Certainly, madam, you shall be accommodated.' I went
with her to Barclay Street; we found him waiting at the door.
He conducted her to Madame Depau's pew, which was vacant.
'I expected to sit in your pew,' she said. 'No, madam,' he replied, 'it would not be proper.' Though he labored under the
disadvantage of speaking a language imperfectly, it being late before he became familiarized with English, he seemed always to
say just what was proper, and what anyone who knew him would
expect him to say. His religion was fervent, sincere, and made
a part of himself; it was never laid aside for worldly purposes.
You must not think from these remarks that Toussaint was a
grave, solemn man; he was full of spirit and animation, and most
entertaining in his little narratives. I have laughed merrily at his
anecdotes and remarks, and when my sister and I were girls, he
used to dance for us as they danced when our parents were young;
and though the style was so different, his attitudes were easy
and graceful. Though very discriminating, and meeting with
amusing things in various families, he was careful never to repeat what passed in different houses, much less to betray the
slightest confidence placed in him. How much I regret that I
cannot be near him at the last! but I have the satisfaction of know-
ing 'all is well.' ''

Many other touching remembrances might be added. One
French lady said: "He dressed my hair for my first Communion; he dressed it for my wedding, and for christenings, for balls
and parties; at burials, in sickness and in trouble, he was always
here."

Another said: "The great fire of 1835 changed our fortunes;
the first person who came to us early the next morning was Toussaint, to proffer his services and sympathy."

There is but little to add to this memorial. When I last saw
Toussaint, I perceived that his days were numbered, that he stood
on the borders of the infinite. He was feeble, but sitting in an
armchair, clad in his dressing-gown, and supported by pillows.
A more perfect representation of a gentleman I have seldom

seen. His head was strewn with the "blossoms of the grave."
When he saw me he was overcome by affecting remembrances,
for we had last met at the funeral obsequies of the friend so dear
to him. He trembled with emotion, and floods of tears fell from
his eyes. "It is all so changed! so changed!" he said, "so lonely!"
He was too weak to converse, but his mind was filled with
images of the past, of the sweet and noble lady to whose notes
we are indebted. The next day I saw him again, and took leave
of him to see him no more in this world. It was with deep feeling I left his house—that house where I had seen the beings he
dearly loved collected. It was a bright summer morning, the last
of May; the windows were open, and looked into the little gar-
den, with its few scattered flowers. There was nobody now I
had ever seen there, but himself—the aged solitary man!

I left the city, and in early June received notes from a friend
who had visited him daily for months. From these I transcribe.

"Toussaint was in bed today; he says it is now the most comfortable place for him, or as he expressed it in French, '*Il ne
peut pas être mieux.*' He was drowsy and indistinct, but calm,
cheerful, and placid—the expression of his countenance truly
religious. He told me he had received the last Communion, for
which he had been earnest, and mentioned that two Sisters of
Charity had been to see him, and prayed with him. He speaks
of the excellent care he receives—of his kind nurse (she is a white
woman)—and said, 'All is well.' He sent me away when he was
tired, by thanking me."

A few days after, I received the following note:

"Excellent Toussaint! he has gone to those he loved. His depar-
ture took place yesterday at twelve o'clock, without pain or
suffering, and without any change from extreme feebleness. I
saw him on Sunday; he was very low, and neither spoke nor
noticed me.

"On Monday, when I entered, he had revived a little, and
looking up, said, '*Dieu avec moi*,'—'God is with me.' When I
asked him if he wanted anything, he replied with a smile, '*Rien
sur la terre*,'—'Nothing on earth.'

"I did not think he was so near the gates of heaven; but on

Thursday, at twelve o'clock, his spirit was released from its load. He has put off his sable livery, and is clothed in white, and stands with 'palms in his hands, among the multitude of nations which no man can number.' How much I shall miss him every day, for I saw him every day, every day!"

The following note is of a still later date:

"I went to town on Saturday, to attend Toussaint's funeral. High Mass, incense, candles, rich robes, sad and solemn music, were there. The Church gave all it could give, to prince or noble. The priest, his friend, Mr. Quinn, made a most interesting address. He did not allude to his color, and scarcely to his station; it seemed as if his virtues as a man and a Christian had absorbed all other thoughts. A stranger would not have suspected that a black man, of his humble calling, lay in the midst of us. He said, 'Though no relative was left to mourn for him, yet many present would feel that they had lost one who always had wise counsel for the rich, words of encouragement for the poor, and all would be grateful for having known him.'

"The aid he had given to the late Bishop Fenwick of Boston, to Father Powers of our city, to all the Catholic institutions, was dwelt upon at large. How much I have learnt of his charitable deeds, which I had never known before! Mr. Quinn said, 'There were few left among the clergy superior to him in devotion and zeal for the Church and for the glory of God; among laymen, none.'

"The body of the church was well filled with men, women, children, nuns, and charity sisters; likewise a most respectable collection of people of his own color, all in mourning. Around stood many of the white race, with their eyes glistening with emotion. When Juliette was buried, Toussaint requested that none of his white friends would follow her remains; his request was remembered now, and respected; they stood back as the coffin was borne from the church, but when lowered to its last depository, many were gathered round his grave."

Thus lived and died Pierre Toussaint; and of him it may be truly said, in the quaint language of Thomas Fuller, an old English divine, that he was "God's image carved in ebony."

APPENDIX

W E insert the following notices, which appeared, among several others, after the death of Toussaint, as they prove how much and how universally he was respected and appreciated.

The following short notice of him appeared the other day [July 2, 1853] in two of the New York morning papers:

"Pierre Toussaint, whose funeral will take place this morning, at ten o'clock, from St. Peter's Church, Barclay Street, was born in the servitude of St. Domingo, and, in devoted attendance upon his mistress in her flight from that island, arrived in this city in 1787. Here the former dependent became the sole support of the unfortunate lady, and her most disinterested friend until her death.

"The occupation of ladies' hair-dresser gave him admission to the houses of the influential families of that day, and his good manners, unusual discrimination of character, and high sense of propriety insured him the countenance, courtesy, and esteem of all to whom he was admitted, and the confidence and friend-ship of many to whom the excellency of his life and character was more intimately known. All knew his general worth, but few were acquainted with the generous qualities of his heart, and with those principles of disinterested and genuine kindness which governed his daily conduct.

"His charity was of the efficient character which did not content itself with a present relief of pecuniary aid, but which required time and thought by day and by night, and long watchfulness and kind attentions at the bedside of the sick and the departing. Thus goodness springing from refined and elevated principle, and from a sense of religious duty, which never permitted him to omit a most scrupulous compliance with all the requirements of his faith, formed the prominent feature of his character, and made his life a constant round of acts of kindness and sympathy.

"By such a life, governed by such principles of integrity, charity, and religion, Toussaint secured to himself the respect, esteem, and friendship of many of our first citizens; and though death has made the circle small in which he had moved, there are yet remaining many who remember his excellence and worth with the kindest appreciation.

"S."

The following is an extract from a notice that appeared in the *New York Evening Post*:

"UNCLE TOM NOT AN APOCRYPHAL CHARACTER—A correspondent suggests to us, that the aged black man, Pierre Toussaint, who came to this city nearly sixty years ago from St. Domingo, and last week closed a long, useful, and blameless life, might, if Mrs. Stowe could have been supposed to have known him, have sat as the original of the portraiture to which she gave the name of Uncle Tom. Toussaint is spoken of by all who knew him as a man of the warmest and most active benevolence, the gentlest temper, and the most courteous and graceful, yet wholly unassuming manners. The successive pastors of St. Peter's Church had all the same opinion of him, and it is said that, when the present pastor came to bury him, he observed that he had not such a man left among his congregation. It would be worth the while of anyone who knew him well, to give in a brief memoir some anecdotes of a life which was, throughout, so shining an example of goodness. . . .

"It is related of a gentleman, formerly of this city, distinguished for the wit and point of his conversation, that he was one day talking with a lady, who instanced Hyde de Neuville as more fully illustrating her idea of a perfect gentleman than any other person she had known. He replied: 'The most perfect gentleman I have ever known is Pierre Toussaint.'"

The following is part of a notice in the *Home Journal*, which, a few days after, proceeded from the pen of Mr. Henry T. Tuckerman:

"Died on Thursday, June 30th, at his residence in this city, Pierre Toussaint, in the eighty-seventh year of his age.

"We cannot allow this brief announcement to form the sole record of one whose example is a higher vindication of his race, or rather a nobler testimony to the beauty and force of character, than all the works of fiction that studious invention ever conceived. Pierre Toussaint for more than sixty years has been the most respected and beloved negro in New York. He came here in 1787, with his mistress. . . . He soon began to exercise his rare talents as a hair-dresser, and became indispensable to the ladies of New York, and their children. A very few of the brides, whose tresses he so daintily arrayed, yet survive; and as long as any of them lived, Pierre paid them regular visits, and was always certain of a kind reception. He supported his beloved mistress, not only in comfort, but luxury, when her means failed, until the day of her death. Meantime, he had associated himself with all the best families. The wives and daughters loved to listen to his tropical reminiscences, or his cheerful comments on the news of the day, as he adorned their heads for the evening party; and the children delighted to put themselves under his kindly hands when the time came for a hair-cutting. Pierre was thus busy from morning to night. . . . After the death of his mistress he married, and was enabled to purchase a very good house in Franklin Street. He retired from business with an adequate fortune, and thenceforth devoted himself to social and benevolent duty. His relations in the former respect were threefold; first, to his cherished lady friends and their families, whom he had attended in youth, and towards whom he exhibited a disinterested and loyal attachment, which seemed to belong to a past age or a different country, so unique and touching was its manifestation; second, to the French population of New York, to which he was attached by early association and native language; and thirdly, to his own race, the mass of whom were so much below him in tone of character and position, that only a fraternal sentiment truly Christian could have prompted his constant interest in their welfare, and ready sympathy in their pleasures and griefs. By these so widely different classes Pierre was both respected and beloved. He moved among them in a way peculiarly his own. He possessed a sense of the appropriate, a self-respect, and a uniformity of demeanor, which amounted to genius. No familiarity ever made him forget what was due to his superiors, and prosperity and reputation never hardened his heart towards the less favored of his own class.

"For sixty years he attended Mass at six in the morning, as punctual as a clock, until prostrated by illness. His days and nights were given to visits, ministrations to the sick, attendance upon the bereaved, and attempts to reform the erring and console the afflicted. . . . Often strangers paused to look with curiosity and surprise upon the singular tableau presented in Broadway of the venerable negro, with both his hands clasped in greeting by a lady high in the circles of fashion or birth, and to watch the vivid interest of both, as they exchanged inquiries for each other's welfare.

"The last time I saw Pierre, he was seated among a group of mourners, beside the coffin of a lady venerated for years in the highest social sphere of the city. She was almost the last tie that bound him to the past. He had visited her daily for thirty years, and brought his offering of flowers; and there he sat, with his white head bowed in grief, and every line of his honest sable face wet with tears. It was a beautiful homage to worth—a beautiful instance of what may be the disinterested relation between

OLD ST. PATRICK'S CATHEDRAL
MOTT ST., NEW YORK CITY

Toussaint was buried beside his wife, Juliette, and his niece, Euphemia, in the cemetery of old Saint Patrick's Cathedral on Mott Street. In 1990 his remains were moved to the new Saint Patrick's Cathedral on Manhattan's Fifth Avenue.

the exalted and the humble—when the genius of character and the sentiment of religion bring them thus together.

"Pierre was buried in the Cathedral churchyard, beside his wife and adopted child; and his funeral was attended by gentlemen and menials, his death-bed soothed by the fairest, as well as venerated by the most humble representatives of the wide circle included in his sympathies and attracted by his worth. Peace to the ashes of good, noble, loyal Pierre Toussaint!"

THE END

LETTERS

[*Letter from Toussaint to William Schuyler*]

57

New York, November 5, 1823

SIR,

I have received your charming letter which has truly afforded me the greatest pleasure in the world and I see well that you
are a young man of word. Yes, my dear sir, I believe I am the
happiest of all mortals when I receive letters from Madame la
Comtesse de Basturd and I assure you indeed that I am quite
proud to receive a letter from Mr. William Schuyler, for I think
and I am certain that you have the feelings of a true nobleman,
that is to say, *d'un homme comme il faut.* Thus if you should
ever marry, and I should have the happiness of receiving a letter from your lady I should consider her the Countess William
Schuyler. All the young men at Mr. Bancel's say a thousand
things to you. Mr. and Mrs. Bancel do not forget you at all. Madame Binsse is doing very well. I did you the favor of present-
ing your regards to those young ladies. They are very sensible
to your pleasant remembrances. Miss Collins is leaving tomor-
row for her home and Miss Marcathy is leaving for Saint Croix
because of her health. ... Mr. Cruger has just arrived, and I
received a very long letter from the Countess that made me

87

happy. I go to your mother's house every day. She is doing very well. Your cousins are always quite well. The young ladies hope to see you this winter at Mr. Bancel's ball. Miss Meetz says thousands and thousands of things to you. Adieu, my good and dear Mr. William, take care of yourself and always be good and write to me some time when time is not pressing. I am respectfully your very obedient servant,

P. TOUSSAINT

[*Letter from Toussaint to his wife, Juliette*]

New York, July 8, 1833

DEAR JULIETTE,

I have received your letter dated the 6th. I am very glad that your apprehension has left you peaceful. Thanks be to God, I am always in good health. Your mother is doing well and all your acquaintances ask me if I have news of you. I have told them that Madame Toussaint is doing very well, thanks be to God, and she is amusing herself a lot with her friends from Baltimore. I thank those gentlemen and ladies for having received you so well. Tell them friendly things, above all to Madame Montpensier. Tell her that I ask her not to spoil you too much and at the same time I urge you to follow her good examples, although I know that you have the very best, one can never have too many. Everyone says hello to you. Francis and Mr. Thomas say many respectful things to you. They are doing very well. Mrs. Schuyler says hello to you. Mr. George was quite surprised that I let you go all alone. I told him that you know well that business always goes before all else, and that my wife is in good company, and that I hope she will amuse herself; this is all my consolation. Tell me if you have listened to sermons in French. Yesterday I had dinner at Mrs. Castane's home. Josephine and her mother tell you a thousand things. She asks you to give her regards to all those ladies. Mrs. Michel and her mother say hello to you. The J__ ladies do not forget you. They send their regards to Mrs. Noel without forgetting Mrs. Montpensier.

Caboisse does not forget anyone. Adieu, dear friend. I send you
a thousand hugs. I am yours,

P. TOUSSAINT

[Letters to Toussaint from his niece, Euphemie]

New York, January 14, 1826

DEAR UNCLE,

I have heard that an Angel appeared to a watchman and told
him that the city of New York was to be destroyed by an earthquake on the nineteenth of this month and some people say that
the Angel appeared with music, but I do not believe it all though
it has terrified some people very much for I know a lady and
her husband that it has made sick.

Adieu, Dear Uncle,
EUPHEMIE TOUSSAINT

New York, January 20, 1826

DEAR UNCLE,

I am very glad that I was not frightened at the report con-
cerning the earthquake. I think they wanted to get the people
out of the city that they might have the chance to steal, but God
did not permit them to succeed in their wickedness.

Adieu, Dear Uncle,
EUPHEMIE TOUSSAINT

New York, September 15, 1826

DEAR UNCLE,

O how happy I feel to think that I am so near to make my
first Communion. My conscience is so clear I hope it will always be the same. We do not deserve the goodness of God, but
He is so good that He pardons all our sins. We are His children.
He loves us and we ought to love Him.

Adieu, Dear Uncle,
EUPHEMIE TOUSSAINT

New York, June 13, 1828

DEAR UNCLE,

I take this opportunity to write you to tell you that Mr. Genvere says that I have but two weeks to read French as well as any one. I am so pleased to hear it that I will study as much as I can. I have changed my verbs. I am now learning the four conjugations that is not difficult for when you know the first the rest are nothing. Dear Uncle, do you know what part of the country Mrs. Bancel is gone and if she is going to stay all summer? Will you be so kind as to excuse me for having so short a letter this week for I began to compose it very late. I hope that next week I will make it up.

Adieu, Dear Uncle,
EUPHEMIE TOUSSAINT

New York, June 27, 1828

DEAR UNCLE,

I wish you happy Birthday and many happy returns and that God will preserve you to see many more. My prayers are offered morning and night up to God [for] your preservation nor are you ever absent in the day from my mind and that God may preserve you and give you every thing you wish . . . until I am able to earn my living. I expect to support you in your old age as you have supported me [since] my youngest ones. I never expect to do enough for you. I am explaining my sentiments to you without affectation or hypocrisy.

Adieu, Dear Uncle,
EUPHEMIE TOUSSAINT

New York, December 20, 1828

DEAR UNCLE,

You know that Mrs. Rochefort's child is dead, she is to be pitied but not the child for it is gone to heaven where there is no suffering to be found. She is an angel and knows not what is sin. Dear Uncle, I have understood that you was very much

pleased with my French letter last week, I hope that you will
always be pleased with them.

Adieu, Dear Uncle,

EUPHEMIE TOUSSAINT

[*Excerpt from a letter to Toussaint from John Sorbieu in Rouen,
France, on May 28, 1821*]

You would have been quite delighted, my dear Toussaint, you
who love the King and the Royal family so much, had you seen
all the hats in the air and had heard all the people cry out during his passing, "Long live the King and all the Royal family,"
on April 30, when the King reviewed the troops, numbering
thirty thousand men. You would have had the same delight the
day after, May first, the day of the baptism, when the King was
at Notre Dame to attend the ceremony; the same cries were heard
along all his passage as well as in the evening when he was at
the Hotel de Ville, where he had a magnificent dinner with the
princes and princesses in attendance with the guests. . . .

[*Other letters to Toussaint*]

MY DEAR TOUSSAINT,
It is to you, comforter of the unfortunate, that I appeal, to
beg you, to plead with you to come to see me in this sad place.
I have written to many persons, but in vain! I beg you to come
and see me. Take a carriage. I will pay the fare. God will repay
you for this kindness which I ask of you. I have many things
to tell you. I beg you, do not fail me. I await you today or tomor-
row, or even later.

Your unhappy friend,

L. EMMERLING

Bellevue Prison

MY DEAR TOUSSAINT,
I perfectly appreciate the deep sentiment of friendship that
led you to render the last sad services to the remains of my poor

father. I have seen that your hand followed the impulse of your heart. Ever since I have known you, you have never let pass an occasion to show your attachment to our family by all the care and all the attention in your power. I assure you also that I am deeply grateful for it and I will never forget it. I will now ask you to afford me a great pleasure, that of accepting the armchair that was in my father's use, the one that my sister Louisa gave him, and keep it as a remembrance of him. I hope that it will not be useless to you, and that you will value it as if it were coming from him, himself and me. Give my regards to Juliette and tell her kind things on my behalf. I consider her very fortunate to have as a husband such a worthy and courageous man, so imbued (I say this without wishing to make compliments, because I write what I think) with the principles of true Christian charity.

Be assured of my deep esteem and my sincere friendship,

L. B. BINSSE

[*Letter from Louis F. Binsse, president of the Board of Trustees of Saint Patrick's Cathedral to Pierre Toussaint, apologizing for an insult by an usher at the church*]

MY DEAR TOUSSAINT,

It would be difficult for me to express to you the grief which has been caused me, by the insult which you have received in the Lord's house. It has given me all the more pain, because, wishing to have order in the Church, it was I who begged this gentleman to be one of the masters of ceremony. This young man is truly very repentant for it, and he has been reprimanded most severely by several of the Trustees.

Everybody knows, my dear Toussaint, that if God by His will, has created you as well as your good wife, with a black skin, by His grace He has made your hearts and souls as white as snow. While many others (and you know them well) to whom God has given a white skin, having repulsed this same grace, have made their souls, and hearts also, as black as coal.

You have been disgusted, my dear friend, by such an insult.

I can easily believe it. I should have been so, as much as you, and perhaps more than you, because you are human and I also. Our divine Master is the only One, Who, insulted, beaten with rods and crucified, submitted Himself with meekness to the will of His Father, when He could, by the breath of His mouth, have crushed His executioners.

What ought we to do then, my dear Toussaint? Imitate Him as much as our weakness and His grace will permit us to do. If by our weakness we resent insult, by His grace it should be forgotten. For my part, I would find myself more at ease, seated in the house of the Lord between you and your wife, and the good Cabresse, than beside many other persons whose skin is as white as satin. In the house of the Lord there is no distinction. God looks at the heart, but never at the color of the skin.

There are the sentiments of all the Trustees, and of him who is most sincerely your friend.

L. F. BINSSE
August 24, 1842

[*Document giving Pierre Toussaint his freedom*]

French Empire
Trusteeship of New York and New Jersey
Extract from the Minutes of the Chancellery of the Trusteeship of France in New York, No. 633
I, the undersigned, Elisabeth Bossard, wife of Monsieur Gabriel Nicolas, declare, with the consent of Monsieur Nicolas, my husband, that my intention is that Pierre Toussaint, my slave, shall be and live free from all servitude and I consent that he enjoy his liberty like any other freeman, and that this present act be given all the public authenticity that it may have. Made in New York on July 2, 1807.
(Signed) Bossard N.
Gabriel N.
Signed and sealed in the presence of
(Signed) John Sorbieu
F. G. Brun

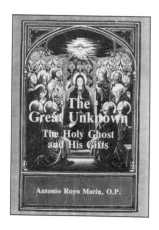